House of Medici

A Captivating Guide to the History of the Medici Family and Dynasty

© Copyright 2021

All Rights Reserved. No part of this book may be reproduced in any form without permission in writing from the author. Reviewers may quote brief passages in reviews.

Disclaimer: No part of this publication may be reproduced or transmitted in any form or by any means, mechanical or electronic, including photocopying or recording, or by any information storage and retrieval system, or transmitted by email without permission in writing from the publisher.

While all attempts have been made to verify the information provided in this publication, neither the author nor the publisher assumes any responsibility for errors, omissions or contrary interpretations of the subject matter herein.

This book is for entertainment purposes only. The views expressed are those of the author alone, and should not be taken as expert instruction or commands. The reader is responsible for his or her own actions.

Adherence to all applicable laws and regulations, including international, federal, state and local laws governing professional licensing, business practices, advertising and all other aspects of doing business in the US, Canada, UK or any other jurisdiction is the sole responsibility of the purchaser or reader.

Neither the author nor the publisher assumes any responsibility or liability whatsoever on the behalf of the purchaser or reader of these materials. Any perceived slight of any individual or organization is purely unintentional.

Free Bonus from Captivating History (Available for a Limited time)

Hi History Lovers!

Now you have a chance to join our exclusive history list so you can get your first history ebook for free as well as discounts and a potential to get more history books for free! Simply visit the link below to join.

Captivatinghistory.com/ebook

Also, make sure to follow us on Facebook, Twitter and Youtube by searching for Captivating History.

Contents

INTRODUCTION 1
CHAPTER 1 – THE RISE OF THE ITALIAN CITY-STATES 3
CHAPTER 2 – FLORENCE BEFORE THE RISE OF THE MEDICI 7
CHAPTER 3 – THE EARLY MEDICI AND COSIMO, THE "FATHER OF THE FATHERLAND" 20
CHAPTER 4 – LORENZO IL MAGNIFICO (LORENZO THE MAGNIFICENT) 43
CHAPTER 5 – THE FIRST MEDICI POPE 87
CHAPTER 6 – THE LAST GREAT MEDICI: CATHERINE 102
CONCLUSION 110
HERE'S ANOTHER BOOK BY CAPTIVATING HISTORY THAT YOU MIGHT LIKE 112
FREE BONUS FROM CAPTIVATING HISTORY (AVAILABLE FOR A LIMITED TIME) 113
BIBLIOGRAPHY 114

Introduction

Before Jeff Bezos, Elon Musk, Bill Gates, Warren Buffet, and Richard Branson, before the Gettys, the Rockefellers, the Vanderbilts, and Rothschilds came the Medicis of Florence. Even if you are not familiar with the name, you are likely familiar with some of the artists they sponsored and the movement of which they were an integral part: the Renaissance.

The Medici family of Florence, Italy, had humble farming roots, but through hard work and incredible business and political acumen, they rose to heights of power and gained riches and influence that was rare to find then and even now. They were bankers, power brokers, patrons of the arts, archbishops, cardinals, and popes. They were perhaps the most influential family in 15th-century Europe, and many of their achievements are still with us today.

The Medici were the patrons of some of the most towering figures of Renaissance and art history, such as Da Vinci, Michelangelo, Botticelli, Brunelleschi, and Donatello, along with dozens of other lesser lights. Perhaps other patrons may have come along had the Medici never existed, but it can be safely said that, in many ways, the Medici were the "Godfathers of the Renaissance." They bankrolled, protected, and promoted some of the greatest minds of their time, which also included the controversial astronomer and scientist Galileo Galilei.

For a time, the Medici were the richest people in Europe, and kings, dukes, and bishops all came to them for loans. At the beginning of their incredible rise, they influenced and ruled Florence from behind the scenes. The later members of the family ruled openly as popes, dukes, and queens.

The Medici were survivors. They survived wars, assassinations, religious revolutions, and the Protestant Reformation (the last of which was indirectly caused by one of the Medici family, Pope Leo X). In this Captivating History edition, we will introduce you to not only Leo X but also his great-grandfather "Cosimo the Great," his father "Lorenzo the Magnificent," and his grand-niece, Catherine de' Medici, Queen Consort of France from 1547 to 1559 and the de facto ruler of the largest country in western Europe from 1560 to 1563. During that time, her eldest son, Francis II, was a child, and she also acted as the power behind the throne during the reigns of her two other sons, Charles IX and Henry III.

As you read about these four powerful people, you will also meet the artists of the Renaissance and a whole cast of characters that will hopefully help bring this amazing period of human history come to life for you.

Chapter 1 – The Rise of the Italian City-States

The Italian Peninsula in 1499. Though borders shifted often, this was generally how Italy was divided at the beginning of the Medicis' rise to power in the late 14th and early 15th centuries.
TheWiseBeluga, CC BY-SA 4.0 <https://creativecommons.org/licenses/by-sa/4.0>, via Wikimedia Commons https://commons.wikimedia.org/wiki/File:Italy_in_1499.png

In the late 400s CE, the Roman Empire, or rather what was left of it, finally fell to the tribes of northern and central Europe, which had been attacking and besieging her for about 150 years. In 476, the partially Romanized Germanic king Odoacer became the first "King of Italy." The year 476 is generally considered the ending point of the Roman Empire and the beginning of what used to be called the Dark Ages.

After Odoacer came Theodoric II, an Ostrogoth who set up his capital in the northeastern city of Ravenna, from where the last Western Roman emperors had attempted to rule. Theodoric and leaders of other Gothic tribes ruled much of the former Western Roman Empire from Italy until the late 500s when another Germanic tribe, the Lombards, conquered much of the Italian Peninsula. (The Roman Empire was divided between the West—centered in Rome—and the East—centered in Constantinople—in the late 300s.) The Kingdom of the Lombards reached its height under Aistulf (r. 749-756). But under pressure from both the armies of the Eastern Roman Empire and the newly emergent Muslim armies in the south, as well as the man who would become the first "Holy Roman Emperor," Charlemagne, in the north, the Lombards faded from history, although they did lend their name to a region of Italy in the north: Lombardy.

Charlemagne and his allies in the Catholic hierarchy, namely Pope Leo III, governed much of Italy from the late 8th century until Charlemagne's death in 814. Charlemagne's will called for the division of his massive empire into three parts—one for each of his sons: Charles, known as "the Bald," even though he apparently had a full head of hair, Lothar, and Louis, sometimes known as "Louis the German." An arrangement was made with the pope and the Catholic Church that gave them rule over a significant portion of Italy.

It was Charlemagne's hope that his sons would be able to get along and work with each other in peace, but that was not to be. They constantly vied with each other for influence, warred with one another at times, and worked to undermine one another throughout their lifetimes. As you can see from the map above, Lothar controlled the important commercial highway of the Rhine River and had access to the North, Mediterranean, and Adriatic Seas, but he was sandwiched between his two powerful brothers. Keeping control of the important parts of his territory along the Rhine while also controlling Italy was more than he and his sons could handle.

By the 2nd century of the new millennium, Italy was in the process of breaking up into a conglomeration of duchies, aristocratic republics, minor kingdoms, and the Papal States. Even within the Papal States, powerful aristocrats, who were sometimes in an alliance with one another and sometimes were on their own, wrested much power from the papacy. In the very south and in Sicily, various powers, from pirates to Muslim caliphs to Norman knights, vied with each other for control.

The Holy Roman emperors, in particular, Frederick I of the House of Hohenstaufen, popularly known as Barbarossa for his red beard, attempted to retain control of the northern part of the Italian Peninsula. In 1176, Barbarossa's forces fought and lost a war against the cities of Lombardy, which, despite the continued unsuccessful attempts of Barbarossa's successors, developed their own complex governments and organizations.

By 1300, what is now Italy was divided into dozens of large and small entities, as shown on the map below.

As you can see, Florence, which is located 176 miles north of Rome, was surrounded by other cities and territories, and it is a long way from the water. On the surface, the city's location would make it difficult for it to continue independently, much less prosper. However, in an age when transportation was limited to walking, horseback riding, or traveling in a wagon in a time with very few serviceable roads and in an area of valleys, steep hills, rivers, and ravines, Florence's location served to protect it from many of the troubles that engulfed other city-states around it.

Florence also possessed another rarity: one of the most financially and politically savvy families in human history.

Chapter 2 – Florence before the Rise of the Medici

Before we tell you about the Medici themselves, it's important to understand the city in which they lived. Without the Medici, there would likely have been no Florentine "Golden Age," and without Florence, there may have been no Medici dynasty.

Unlike the vast majority of European states, which were ruled by what became known as the feudal system, in which an aristocratic lord governed the lands under his control more or less as he saw fit, many of the Italian states of central and northern Italy developed along different lines.

Though some called themselves or are referred to as "republics," a more accurate description might be "proto-republics." Though these governments were infinitely more representative of the people that they governed, especially when compared to the feudal states of northern and eastern Europe, they more closely resembled the early English parliamentary system or the first century and a half of the United States.

Many people who would not have been represented (not to mention having a vote) in the rest of Europe, such as small independent farmers, urban workers, and merchants, did have some voice if they lived in one of the aforementioned Italian city-states, especially in Florence. It is likely that this form of government allowed the Italian city-states (especially Florence, Genoa, and Venice) to punch way above their weight and size, both economically and politically, compared to the larger states of Europe.

Not all but much of this was due to the small size of these city-states. At a time when both communication and transportation were dependent on the speed on which a human being, horse, or perhaps slow-moving ship could travel, a smaller state was much easier to govern than a larger one. The anarchy and almost constant internal warfare experienced by the larger European states, while existent in the Italian states, was, generally speaking, not as bloody and prolonged as the conflicts in the north.

The political structure of France, for example, was a top-down government that worked something like the following. At the top was the king (or sometimes a queen, as in Elizabethan England, or both as in Columbus's Spain under Ferdinand and Isabella). Below him were the various dukes and princes, who were usually his brothers, cousins, or other close family members. These dukes would govern major regions (for example, the powerful region of Aquitaine in the southwest). These regions might have been further broken down into smaller provinces, each governed by one of the duke's men, who might have had the title of "duke" or perhaps a lesser one such as "baron" or "count." These men might have ruled a city or smaller region within the province and, like the dukes and princes above them, were responsible for gathering taxes from the people—much of which (theoretically) was supposed to make it to the king. Many families owned large tracts of land within the province, and at each of these levels (again, generally speaking), they would have had complete control of his/her land and the people within it as long as they paid their taxes and turned up with men under arms when summoned by their lords, whether that was the king or the local duke.

The only political rival to the monarch's power was the Catholic Church and, after the Reformation of the late 1500s/early 1600s, the various Protestant councils or bishops who arose in various localities in England, the states of Germany, Scandinavia, and Holland. Before the Reformation (especially in the period of the Medici family's rise in the late 1200s), the Catholic Church was almost all-powerful throughout western and northern Europe. A delicate balance between church and state existed, and it sometimes failed, giving way to political murder, manipulation, and sometimes outright war.

This happened in fits and starts between 1125 and 1186 and 1216 and 1392 (the latter is the period we are most concerned with here). These wars, which were between supporters of the Holy Roman emperors and the popes, are referred to as the Guelph and Ghibelline Wars.

In the 1100s, two German families vied for power and the position of Holy Roman emperor. These were the supporters of Frederick I Barbarossa and Frederick II (a distant relative of the former) of the German principality of Swabia (in today's southwestern Germany). The name "Ghibelline" is the Italian form of the German name "Waiblingen," the ancient castle of the powerful dukes of Swabia.

The Guelphs were originally made up of Bavarian opponents to the House of Swabia and were supported by the pope, who believed they could be more easily controlled (the Ghibellines believed in the primacy of the Holy Roman emperor in all things outside the church). The word "Guelph," or "Guelfi," was the Italianized form of the name of an ancient territorial dynasty, the "Welf."

Of course, like most wars, the Guelph and Ghibelline Wars, especially the second one, devolved into a conflict between not just the Holy Roman emperors and their supporters on one side and those of the pope on the other but also territorial rivals who threw in their support to whatever side seemed either to be winning or which offered more for their aid.

In this way, many of the Italian city-states, which had much more in common with each other than with either the papacy or the forces of the Holy Roman Empire (many of whom were from one of the hundreds of German states or dynasties), went to war with one another. Usually, these conflicts between city-states were less about supporting one side or the other and more about what they could gain from their local rivals in terms of territory, agricultural land, influence, treasure, and other economic gains, such as trading rights.

In the 1220s, Florence found itself at war with the cities of Siena (famous for its rough-and-tumble bi-annual horse race, the Palio di Siena, which is still run today), and Pisa (famous for its Leaning Tower). During this time, Florence and its aristocratic leaders were making a push for control of a large part of Tuscany, the rich region in which it and the other cities lay.

Even within cities, there were sometimes divisions between Guelphs and Ghibellines. This was especially true in Florence. In the latter half of the 1200s, factional warfare took place in Florence. With aid from the cities of Siena, Pisa, and Pistoia, the Ghibellines took Florence and ruled it for six years. In 1266, the Guelphs of Florence, with help from French forces, took control. Three years later, the Ghibellines were back.

Beginning in the first years of the 1300s, the Guelphs in Florence split into factions, with one side being the Black Guelphs, who supported Pope Boniface VIII, and the other side being the White

Guelphs, who opposed him. In this struggle, the Black Guelphs won. One of the Whites was a man named Dante Alighieri, the author of the famous *Divine Comedy*, one of the greatest works of literature, not only of its time but in human history. Dante, a Florentine, was exiled, never to see his city again.

Before the time of the Second Guelph-Ghibelline War, the districts of Florence were represented by eight consuls, and there were two or three per district. These consuls worked in conjunction with students of law known as *causidisi*. The consuls were elected by land-owning nobles and wealthy merchants. Here, you can see that, while ahead of its time, especially compared to France and other areas of western Europe, Florentine "democracy" was hardly representative of the entire population. Still, the inclusion of merchants was a step in the right direction, and it was rare in Europe at the time.

However, under the consuls was a council of anywhere between 100 and 150 members, all men. (Here, we must stop and say that unless specifically mentioned, the government and voting population of the city, as in most of Europe at the time, consisted of men only.) Most of the members of this council were not members of the nobility but rather merchants, larger farmers, etc. This "Council of Consuls" could deliberate and consult the consuls but had no final power to make decisions.

At the very bottom of the political structure was the Arengo, which was the popular assembly that met quarterly in a Florentine convent. This assembly ratified the consuls' actions, approved treaties, and confirmed the rights of each of the legislative bodies above it.

Throughout the period of the Second Guelph-Ghibelline War and into the 1300s, Florence became the site of increasing factional fighting and corruption, which sometimes turned to bloodshed. The city was controlled by either ancient noble families or wealthy merchants, and a few of the wealthier farming families began to form alliances and vie with one another for power, riches, and influence in the city.

To a large extent, the center of Florence became a series of fortified houses, palaces, and towers, which protected those inside and symbolized the power of one faction/family. Even while they continued to vie with each other for power and control, the powerful nobility and wealthy merchant class knew that such infighting would inevitably weaken both their position and the city.

Back in the 1100s, Florence and other Italian city-states named a podesta, which comes from an ancient Latin term for "power" or "authority"—*potestas*. This executive was supposed to inject some impartiality into Florentine politics. However, as you might imagine, the podesta, who was selected by one or two of the political bodies mentioned above, always came from a wealthy and/or powerful faction. Thus, they would soon begin to make decisions based on familial or factional loyalty, not the best interests of the city.

It's a tribute to the Florentines that even those who benefited from this situation knew it was untenable, and soon (the mid-to-late 1100s), it was decided that the podesta would come from outside the city. In 1240, the Florentines drew up the *Liber de regimine civitatum*, or "Book of City Management," which, among other things, regulated the behavior and power of the podesta.

When the person the council wanted to serve was identified and agreed upon, they then had to ask the city for permission. This was done through a vote, and men whose families had lived in the city and its immediate surroundings for at least three generations and who owned land would take part. If this was received (and it usually was), the candidate for the job was contacted about his pay and when his time in office would begin. If an agreement was reached, on the day his tenure was to begin, there was a swearing-in ceremony in front of the city's bishop and a gathering of armed citizens.

As another safeguard against the podesta being swayed or bribed to act one way or another, his contact with the people was proscribed. Everywhere he went, he was accompanied by seven rectors (representatives of the major guilds in Florence), and he was not even allowed to go out to eat.

In addition to the position of the podesta, the Florentine government had several checks and balances built into it, at least before the rise of the Medici in the early 1400s. Other civic bodies had a modicum of political and economic power as well. These were the guilds, best thought of for our purposes here as an early form of a labor union.

In Florence, the guilds, or *Arti*, were divided into three sections: the major guilds, the middle guilds, and the minor guilds. The major guilds, or *Arti Majori*, were the judges, notaries, merchants, money-changers, wool traders, physicians, apothecaries (druggists), silk weavers, and furriers/tanners. The middle guilds (*Arti Mediane*) were butchers, graziers (cattlemen), blacksmiths, shoemakers, master stonemasons and wood-carvers, linen manufacturers, retail cloth sellers, and tailors. The minor guilds (*Arti Majori*) were vintners, innkeepers, olive oil and provisions dealers (cheesemakers, candle makers, soap makers, rope makers, etc.), saddle and harness makers, locksmiths, toolmakers, armorers, swordsmiths, carpenters, bakers, and millers. For public events and in some negotiations, this guild structure was used to set precedence, and especially in the minor guilds, movement between "ranks" was common, especially in the minor guilds.

Oddly enough, in a city that was to become famous throughout the "known world" for its art and artists, painters did not have their own guild. They belonged to the guild of doctors and apothecaries (painters bought their paints and pigments from apothecaries). Sculptors belonged to the guild of master stonemasons and woodcarvers. Sculptors who worked in metal belonged to the guild of blacksmiths.

The head of each guild was a captain or *gonfaloniere* ("standard-bearer"). In the 1400s, the name of gonfaloniere was given to a new chief executive as well. Each guild had a headquarters, standard, and political structure.

In the 13th and 14th centuries, the growth of the non-aristocratic middle class greatly increased the popularity and power of the guilds, and it also gave rise to yet another political structure: "the people" (in Latin, *populo*). Though the name makes it sound as if the common people were the leaders of this group, they were not. Rather, the middle class and wealthy merchants dominated it. Still, the *populo* did give the common people some voice through its wealthy and more influential members and in the choice of some of the neighborhood leaders.

In Renaissance Florence, the *populo* were divided into twenty sections or "companies," which represented the number of neighborhoods in the city. Each group had a gonfaloniere, who was aided by four rectors. They were elected by a council of twenty-four men, who were, in turn, elected by the members of each company. In times of war, the Florentine militia was divided along company lines.

Lastly, the "people" as a whole were led by a captain (*capitano*). This man could order the ringing of the bell in the Tower of the Leoni ("Lions") near the Ponte Vecchio (one of Florence's most recognized landmarks) in the center of the city when there was trouble. He also accompanied the podesta in public events as the "people's representative."

The Ponte Vecchio today. It appears almost exactly as it did in the time of the Medici.
Rufus46, CC BY-SA 3.0 <https://creativecommons.org/licenses/by-sa/3.0>, via Wikimedia Commons https://commons.wikimedia.org/wiki/File:Ponte_Vecchio_Westen_Florenz-10.jpg

As you can see, the government of Florence before, during, and just after the Guelph-Ghibelline Wars was exceedingly rare for the time. As with any system, there were times when it did not function as it was intended, but considering the time and the nature of the governments in most of Europe at the time, the governmental structure was a remarkably early example of the evolution of republican/representative government.

After the chaos of the Second Guelph-Ghibelline War and the civil strife that occurred in Florence during the conflict, Florence's representative form of government, which had served it well in the two centuries before the war, began to change.

Democracy works very well in peacetime. In war, crises and emergencies require swift action that is sometimes lacking in a government that is bogged down by bureaucracy or too many institutions, especially if none of them have a defined role in an emergency situation. Additionally, democracy (or at least what passed for it in Florence at the time) moved slowly, even in peacetime. While consensus is generally good at avoiding internal conflicts, it often moves very slowly. The growing Florentine middle class was also chomping at the bit for more political power as their economic power grew.

In other Italian city-states, some of which had governmental structures similar to that of Florence, a new political body arose: the Signoria, which was based on the power of one family and its head, the signore. This was very similar to the structure of what we call the Mafia.

In Florence, the Signoria took a different form. There were nine members called Priors (*Priori*); six were from the major guilds, and two were from the minor. At first, these men served for two months, but it was discovered that this was impracticable and changed to six. A gonfaloniere was chosen to represent them only at certain important functions and events.

In Florence, a confusing array of new political bodies replaced the structures in place before and during the Second Guelph-Ghibelline War. The Priors were obliged to consult with two other bodies: the Twelve Good Men (*Dodici Buonomini*) and the Sixteen Gonfaloniere (*Sedici Gonfalonieri*). Other political bodies included the *Otto di Guardia* (whose name in both English—the "Eight of Ward"—and Italian belies its function: the secret police), and the *Sei di Commercio* ("Six of Commerce"), which monitored economic activity in and around the city.

In times of war or imminent hostility, two-thirds of the vote was required to form an emergency body known as the *Dieci di Balia*, or the "Ten of War," which was most likely composed of experienced soldiers and powerful men. The Ten of War were given emergency power only during times of conflict.

Throughout the 1300s, Florence was the scene of much violence, political chaos, and change. The changes that gave birth to the aforementioned structures involved attempts by foreign rulers to exercise a one-man rule over Florence.

Toward the end of the Black and White Guelph power struggle in Florence, the Guelph king of Naples, Robert of Anjou (sometimes known as "Robert the Wise," the most powerful man in Italy and whose father's family had roots and vast lands in France as well), marched into Florence in 1313, ostensibly to put an end to the factional fighting in the city. The elders of the city offered Robert the position of signore, which he accepted. Robert ruled Florence for about five years, but he was more concerned with growing his kingdom than in governing a small Italian province. Thus, the city managed to avoid the dangers of a one-man rule and feudalism.

However, in 1325, Robert's son, Charles of Calabria (a city in southern Italy), was invited by the Florentines to serve as their military captain and governor for ten years when it was threatened by the leader of a nearby city, Lucca. Charles wasted no time in asserting his firm control over the city, and it looked as if he was trying to set himself up as the permanent signore of Florence. However, he died in 1328, just two months after the leader of the hostile Lucchese (the people of Lucca) passed away.

Once again, in 1342, the city was under threat, and the Florentines asked a well-known military man and mercenary, Walter of Brienne (a city near Toulouse, France), to contractually take power for a year until the threat was dealt with. Walter attempted to break his contract after a year and set himself up as the dictator of Florence, but that was too much for the Florentines. They rose up against him and sent him running from the city in June 1343.

Things remained relatively calm for thirty-five years. In 1378, the Ciompi Revolt happened. The Ciompi were the poor, salaried wool workers of Florence who were at the bottom rung of one of the minor guilds. Not only were the minor guilds essentially pushed aside, but within the guild, the Ciompi were the lowest of the low. They were poor workers who had no power at all. "Ciompi" is like the English word "clomp," for these people were named for the sound their wooden shoes made on the pavement.

From 1375 to 1378, Florence was involved in a war that pitted it against the forces of Pope Gregory XI, who was attempting to forcibly increase the size of church lands. Although Florence had forced out the anti-Pope Ghibellines years before, Pope Gregory XI's move to take over the city was too much. War ensued between Gregory and his allies and the Florentines and their allies, which were facing the same threat.

A series of confusing ordinances were passed in Florence that took power from a large number of former rich Guelph families. They had moved from the countryside into Florence at the start of the 1300s, and it was believed they supported Gregory. By 1378, this amounted to the majority of the wealthy families in Florence. In June of that year, one of the city's leaders, Gonfaloniere Salvestro de' Medici (who belonged to what is known to history as the secondary and less illustrious branch of the Medici), fired up the minor guilds and its workers, many of whom were the Ciompi of the wool guild. On June 21st, violence broke out throughout the city between the Ciompi and their supporters in the minor guilds and those of the middle class and the major guilds. In July, it appeared that the Ciompi and the minor guilds had won, and they formed a new political structure in which each minor guild was given a place in government.

The head of this new government was a man named Michele di Lando. Between July and the end of August, the two sides in the conflict waged an economic and political war with one another. The merchants and middle class initiated a lockout, which prevented the workers from attending their jobs, and the new government of the minor guilds passed laws that gave more rights and votes to the masses and not just those at the top of the economic, political, and social order.

By the end of August, infighting within the ranks of the Ciompi and minor guilds had begun, with the more radical among them calling for a complete restructuring of Florence's government. Di Lando and the more conservative elements in the movement then approached the merchants and middle class with a plan. On August 31st, di Lando called for a mass demonstration in the main square of Florence, the Piazza della Signoria. Hundreds of Ciompi arrived, but they found that all the exits to and from the piazza were blocked. The forces of the middle class, along with hired mercenaries, slaughtered virtually all of them.

With the fall of the Ciompi, Florence entered a new phase, one dominated by wealthy families. One emerged above all the others as the clear leader of the city: the Medici. And this could be seen in the ascent of an amazing man named Cosimo de' Medici, also known as "Cosimo the Elder."

Chapter 3 – The Early Medici and Cosimo, the "Father of the Fatherland"

The name "Medici" means "physicians," but there is no evidence that any of the early family members practiced medicine. There was a legend among the family and in Florence that a long-ago ancestor of the Medici was indeed a doctor and that the six red balls on a field of gold on the family crest represented pills of some kind. However, pills, as we know them, were not developed for some time after the ascent of the Medici. Many people believed that the crest actually symbolized medieval Byzantine weights called *bisanti*, which were used as a standard of measurement by merchants and bankers.

Medici family crest at the time of Cosimo I. The crest changed as the fortunes of the family grew.
Oren neu dag, Dbachmann, CC BY-SA 2.0 <https://creativecommons.org/licenses/by-sa/2.0>, via Wikimedia Commons
https://commons.wikimedia.org/wiki/File:Coat_of_Arms_of_Medici_unaugmented.svg

In the 1300s, a man named Averardo de' Medici served as a gonfaloniere, but at the time, the Medici was likely a family of woolmakers and traders who, while successful, did not come close to amassing the riches of their descendants. His grandson, also named Averardo, began to amass a real fortune, especially for traders. The elder Averado's great-grandson, Giovanni di Bicci de' Medici (b. 1360), was the first to amass what could be considered a "fortune," and he was also the first of what became known as the "first branch" of the Medici, from which Cosimo sprung. Another branch, known as the "secondary branch," contained later popes and other influential figures.

When Giovanni was three, his father died, and his will divided his fortune among his four sons. Since Giovanni was an infant, he received little. In an era where the wealthy only lived to about fifty years old, children began to work or apprentice early. So, probably around the age of thirteen, Giovanni was apprenticed to an uncle,

Vieri de' Medici, who ran a money-changing business and financed trading ventures along the eastern Adriatic coast. Vieri later entered into joint partnerships with three of his nephews, Giovanni, who was based in Rome, being one of them. Giovanni must have done well, as he established a wide circle of business clients and contacts, as well as personal friends and acquaintances, for reasons that will become apparent shortly.

In 1393, Vieri retired and went into political life, becoming the Gonfaloniere of Justice; however, he only lived two years after his retirement from the business. Upon his retirement, his business was divided between his nephews. The banks run by Giovanni's two cousins eventually dissolved, one shortly after starting and another in the mid-1400s. Of the three, Giovanni was the most successful, and he founded the Medici Bank in 1397.

In addition to his bank, which had branches not only in northern Italy but also in France, the Netherlands, England, and Germany, Giovanni had the family's wool business. He was also a member of two guilds in Florence: banking and wool trading (one way of gaining political power was membership in a number of guilds). Giovanni, along with a number of other influential members of the city, began to patronize the arts, especially the civic arts (art that would benefit the city at large). Some examples are the now-famous bronze depictions on the Florence Baptistery. These influential men would have also been acquainted with the soon-to-be-famous architect Filippo Brunelleschi and Donato di Niccolo di Betto Bardi, better known to history as the master sculptor Donatello.

Giovanni de' Medici.
https://commons.wikimedia.org/wiki/File:Bronzino-Giovanni-di-Medici-cropped.jpg

    The Medici family was becoming powerful and influential even before the rise of Giovanni and his even more powerful son, Cosimo. As you have read, a distant relative named Salvestro de' Medici supported the Ciompi Revolt. For his part, Giovanni also played to the masses, most of whom, then like now, lived paycheck to paycheck (or "florin to florin" as it was in the 1400s). Giovanni knew that support among the masses could translate into political power in troubled times. To that end, in 1427, Giovanni, as gonfaloniere, pushed forward an income tax in addition to the poll or head tax that each head of the family paid for its members. This early income tax, or catasto, amounted to half of 1 percent of a family's income. This was hardly onerous, but it hit the rich much harder than the poor. As you can probably guess, this made Giovanni many enemies who were determined to bring down the House of Medici.

Luckily for Giovanni, he had two aces up his ample Renaissance sleeves. One was the fact that he had spent his time in Rome getting to know the power players. For thirty-nine years (from 1378 to 1417), the Catholic Church experienced what is known as the Western Schism. The story of the Western Schism is too long for our purposes here, but suffice it to say that the office of pope was not only a religious but also a political one, and men fought for the chance to wield such power. At the time, this usually meant one powerful Italian family and their allies against another family and their allies. One result of the Western Schism was the existence of two popes: one in Rome and the other in Avignon, France. Toward the end of the schism, there was even a third pope based in Pisa, Italy.

In the end, the Council of Constance (1414–1418) was called to resolve the schism and the problems and troubles it brought. The Roman and Pisan popes were forced to abdicate, and the Avignon pope was excommunicated (removed from the church completely).

In this struggle for power in the Catholic Church, Giovanni had backed the winner, who became Pope Martin V. With the ascent of Martin, the Medici Bank won the prize of prizes in medieval banking; it became the banker to the Catholic Church. Not only that, but Giovanni also managed to secure the friendship of the Pisan "antipope" (as the former non-Roman popes of the schism were later called). One can easily see his skill in balancing personality and power.

In the later years of his life, which was a long one by the standards of the time (sixty-eight), Giovanni entered politics and began endowing projects for the betterment of Florence, particularly his neighborhood near the Basilica. In 1417, the plague struck Florence, and Giovanni was one of the few rich men in the city to help the poor through it. He also played an important role in a children's hospital, which was designed by Brunelleschi. It was actually Giovanni who pushed Brunelleschi forward as the architect for Florence's most recognizable landmark and the architect's crowning glory: the Dome of Santa Maria del Fiore Cathedral.

By the time of his death in 1428, Giovanni had laid the foundations of the coming Medici dynasty in Florence. The Medici was the most powerful family in Florence and perhaps in Italy for over a century after his death. They were loved by many for their good works and their patronage of the arts. They were also hated by many for their power and the lengths they sometimes took to keep it, as well as by families eager to supplant them as the foremost family in Florence.

Cosimo the Great

Cosimo de' Medici was born in 1389, and for the first forty years of his life, he learned a valuable lesson: how to move behind the scenes and not draw attention to himself. After all, he lived the first part of his life in the shadow of his father, Giovanni.

Cosimo learned at his father's knee, with his responsibilities gradually expanding as he grew older. By the time he married at the age of twenty-five, he was well-traveled, relatively well-known, and well-thought-of. By all accounts, Cosimo was sort of a Renaissance-era Warren Buffet, the latter of whom, despite his immense wealth, lives in the same unassuming home in Omaha that he bought in 1958. However, we must take some of Cosimo's reputation with a grain of salt, as most sources make Cosimo out to be a humble, hard-working man who had some of the very same habits of businessmen today, including rising early every morning and going to his office.

In his young life, he had an illegitimate child by a slave girl. Likely, family chastisement and his own religious beliefs, plus a concern for his image as well as maturity, put an end to this. By all accounts, Cosimo was the picture of the "family man" for the rest of his life. In his off-time, he planted vineyards and pruned his fruit trees. He dressed modestly, and he was never seen drunk or partaking of too much food at the many politically/economically motivated banquets he threw or were thrown in his honor. People who were invited to the family home were almost always amazed at the difference between his private dining habits and the feasts he hosted for other prominent men, women, and families.

According to contemporary accounts, Cosimo was a humane, forgiving, mild, and quiet man. Of course, he was the head of one of the wealthiest families in Europe as well, so Cosimo must have had a ruthless side, especially since he lived in Florence in the early 1400s. We do know, however, that he valued his anonymity and preferred to move quietly behind the scenes.

In order to have his family and continue the family business, Cosimo had to marry, and his marriage could not be to just anyone. Most likely, he did marry for love; by all accounts, he remained loyal after his marriage. In 1422, he married Contessina de' Bardi, a daughter of what had been the richest family in Florence until they made a tremendously bad business decision.

In the late 1330s, the king of England, Edward III, began what became known as the Hundred Years' War with France in an attempt to assert what he believed was his rightful claim to the throne of France. In order to do this, Edward not only needed to raise taxes on his people but also secure loans. The amount of money he needed was so immense that he needed to secure loans from banks both inside England and outside it. Two of the places where he got large loans were from the Bardi and Peruzzi families of Florence, which at the time were Florence's leading banking families.

Unfortunately for the Bardi and Peruzzi families, when Edward III defaulted on his massive loans, they had no means by which to collect. Two small families in Florence, Italy (750 miles from England as the crow flies), were never going to force the king of England to pay them back. So, they went bankrupt.

Moving into the void was Cosimo de' Medici, whose Medici Bank now became the largest in Florence. It would soon be the largest in Europe. By marrying Contessina de' Bardi, Cosimo was making allies and helping a soon-to-be-destitute family save face. Additionally, the Medici bought the Casa di Bardi, the ancestral home of the Bardi family, which was where Cosimo and his wife lived until the death of Cosimo's father, Giovanni. Their firstborn son, Piero (known to history as "Piero the Gouty" for the illness that he and many other of the Medici suffered from), was born there. Contessina's father was made a junior partner in the Medici business to sweeten the pot and further solidify a new alliance.

Portrait of Cosimo by Bronzino, c. 1545, based on an earlier portrait.
https://commons.wikimedia.org/wiki/File:Cosimo_di_Medici_(Bronzino).jpg

After Giovanni's death, Cosimo and his family moved into a new residence—actually, it was a palace that Cosimo had been building for some time. This was the Palazzo Medici, known today as the Palazzo Medici Riccardi for the family that purchased it in the late 1600s. Today, the palace is located within the city of Florence, crammed between other buildings and the seat of the Florentine government, as well as a museum. However, when Cosimo moved in, the palace was surrounded by land, as well as security features. The palace was designed by Michelozzo di Bartolomeo Michelozzi, who was not only one of the greatest architects of the time but also a personal friend of Cosimo, remaining so in good times and bad.

The building of the palace presented a problem for Cosimo. His family was not of the nobility; actually, many of the old noble families of Florence considered the Medici part of the common people or perhaps what some today might call the *nouveau riche* ("new rich," a derogatory term for those with more money than taste and manners). At the time, this was more serious than it might be today. In some circles today, being *nouveau riche* might find some doors surprisingly closed to you, but in Renaissance Florence and many other parts of Europe (and for a considerable amount of time afterward), behaving, dressing, and housing oneself or family above one's "station" was a violation of the law. These were called sumptuary laws, and they were even on the books in some American colonies before the American Revolution.

For Cosimo, the stakes were high. He had become one of the richest men in the city, and there were many who were eager to see him and his family displaced and taught a lesson. When he originally thought of the palace, he called in the man who was recognized as the most brilliant (and difficult) architect in Florence, Filippo Brunelleschi, who is today considered to be the father of Renaissance architecture.

As a rule, Cosimo preferred casting an image of humility and reservation, but in the case of the family home, he knew that appearances were sometimes everything. He also was a lover of the arts, so he wanted his home to reflect both the rising influence of his family and his patronage of the arts in Florence. This was not only personally pleasing to him but was also very clearly made to overawe potential and current clients, as well as potential and current enemies.

The problem with Brunelleschi's design was that it was *too* impressive. Brunelleschi's palace, should it have been built, would have been enormous, far beyond the standards of the day and far beyond Cosimo's stated and unstated goals. Should Cosimo have allowed the palace to be built, he would have angered not only the nobility and other wealthy families but also the people of Florence.

Though Florence was fast becoming one of the richest cities in Italy (and Europe), most people were still desperately poor. Cosimo had placed himself as a "man of the people" by funding not only the foundling hospital but also the city's first library and a number of other civic projects. Throughout Cosimo's life and into the life of his son Lorenzo, the common people would come to the offices of the Medici and often meet with Cosimo (or Lorenzo), seeking a favor. Usually, they came with a gift, perhaps cheese or wine, if they were in those trades, or game of some kind for the Medici table. Most often, they would come away from the meeting with, at the very least, a promise that their concerns would be looked into. If you remember the *Godfather* movies, this is how Don Corleone operates—a favor for a favor. In the case of Cosimo, these favors were usually not called in, except when he and the family needed the support of the people to move a project or a Medici-sponsored political move forward.

Alienating the common people by building too grand a palace was out. The people would expect something special in which they could take pride, as they knew their patron was a man of power, prestige, and taste. But "too much was too much"; it was a fine but unwritten line.

As for the nobility, almost anything extravagant would have been a case of a commoner trying to live above his station. Despite the fact that Cosimo ultimately awarded the contract to Michelozzi, whose plans were much more in line with Cosimo's thinking, the nobles of the city, who were already concerned that Cosimo was gaining too much power and influence, used the palace as an excuse to attack him.

In the late 1420s, Florence was dominated by the Albizzi, a family of noblemen who had played a role in Florence's government for at least a century. As Cosimo became richer and more influential and as his palace began to go up, the head of the Albizzi, Rinaldo, began to protest Cosimo's elevation of himself and his family as being beyond their station.

Rinaldo degli Albizzi had allies outside of the city, as he had served in Florence's diplomatic corps. He had also led Florentine forces when they put down a rebellion in the nearby city of Volterra (1428), which had been annexed by Florence in the 13th century. Albizzi also had gotten into trouble with the Florentine authorities for embarking on a war with the nearby city of Lucca, which he started on some flimsy pretext. Though the Florentines took the city, Albizzi was recalled to Florence for personally enriching himself by ordering the sack of Lucca, which had been forbidden.

In order to both maintain his family's influence and keep down the rising Medici, Albizzi convinced a number of other noble families to attack the Medici in any way they could. The easiest and less costly way was to accuse Cosimo of violating the sumptuary laws. This was no joke; when Cosimo was finally put on trial, it was possible that the Gonfaloniere of Justice (who was in the Albizzis' pocket) could sentence Cosimo to death.

For some years, the Albizzi and other nobles' attempts to exile the Medici were blocked by another powerful noble and ally of the Medici, Niccolo da Uzzano. But after Uzzano died in 1431, the Albizzi and their allies made their move. In September of 1433, Cosimo was taken under guard to the Palazzo Vecchio, which was, then as now, Florence's city hall. The ultimate fate for violating the sumptuary laws, especially when they were being applied by your enemy, was death. And not just any death—the violator would be thrown from the highest window of the Palazzo Vecchio's tower to show other Florentines what happened when someone "reached too high." It just so happened that Cosimo was jailed in the cell where that window looked down on the town's main square.

Cosimo's other fear was poison, which was perhaps the most favored method of assassination in Renaissance Italy. Surprisingly, Cosimo was granted permission to receive food from home, and it was brought by a guard who was uncommonly kind to the head of the Medici, a guard who was surely bribed and who likely spread money about on behalf of Cosimo when he wasn't on the job.

The Albizzi and their allies pushed for the death sentence, but this was halted by the appeal of a popular and influential monk named Ambrogio Traversari. He is honored by some Italian Catholics as a saint to this day for his good works and support of the pope in the 1400s, at a time when the church was rocked by conflict. The penalty passed down to Cosimo was twenty years of living in exile.

The Palazzo Vecchio appears much the same today as it did in the time of Cosimo.
*JoJan, CC BY-SA 3.0 <http://creativecommons.org/licenses/by-sa/3.0/>, via Wikimedia Commons
https://commons.wikimedia.org/wiki/File:Firenze_Palazzo_della_Signoria,_better_known_as_the_Palazz
o_Vecchio.jpg*

Cosimo and his entire family (including brothers, nephews, nieces, etc.) naturally had to leave the Palazzo Medici, and they made their first brief stop in the city of Padua, about 140 miles northeast of Florence near the famous city of Venice, which was where they made their temporary home.

Other than avoiding death by impact with the main square of Florence, Cosimo's exile had another benefit. Many people believed that Cosimo might arrange for his own escape and fight the other families in open warfare. If he had been killed, his family certainly would have gone to war. By accepting exile, Cosimo spared Florence a costly war, one that would have cost not only lives but also treasure. After his acceptance of exile, some other noble families began to change their opinion of Cosimo and the Medici, even if just slightly. For their part, the poor in and around Florence were thankful, for they likely would have made up the armies of the rival factions and would have sustained, by far, the most casualties.

Of course, Cosimo did not simply accept his exile and retire into comfortable anonymity in Venice. In addition to bringing the Florentine branch of the Medici Bank with him, he also spread the wealth, knowing that money well invested, whether in property or bribes, often pays for itself many times over, especially at a time when laws were honored in the breach. This caused many influential people and businesses to leave Florence and join Cosimo in Venice.

Cosimo's twenty-year exile lasted only one year. While he was gone, Florence was essentially run by Rinaldo degli Albizzi. He went to war with the powerful Duchy of Milan. The war went poorly for Albizzi. That, combined with the tremendous exit of money from Florence due to Cosimo and his influence, caused the Signoria to call back Cosimo and exile Albizzi instead. During his exile, Albizzi turned on Florence and approached the duke of Milan to return him to power in Florence once the war was won. Unfortunately for Albizzi, the tide turned for Florence, and at the Battle of Anghiari in 1440, the Florentines and their allies defeated Milan. This was in no small part due to Cosimo de' Medici, who had approached the experienced and powerful mercenary Francesco Sforza to lead the Florentine forces, along with a sizable mercenary force. This was all paid for and equipped by the Medici.

In 1505, Leonardo da Vinci was commissioned to create a painting commemorating Florence's victory at Anghiari. He never painted it, but he did create a sketch, seen here.
https://commons.wikimedia.org/wiki/File:Peter_Paul_Ruben%27s_copy_of_the_lost_Battle_of_Anghiari.jpg

Some years later, the now-famous political scientist, Niccolo Machiavelli (who at one time worked with the Medici, then against them, and then with them again) wrote an account of Cosimo's return from exile: "Rarely has it occurred that a citizen, returning triumphant from a victory, was received by the fatherland with such a gathering of people and with such an outpouring of benevolence."

Of course, Machiavelli was a Medici employee at one time, and he admired the family even when opposed to them, so this must be taken with a grain of salt. Regardless, within a very short time, Cosimo went from being an exile to being *the* power in Florence, though he held no official position. Cosimo was careful to work behind the scenes, never drawing too much attention to himself. Though the city was ostensibly still a republic, everyone in power knew that it was wise to run things by Cosimo before moving forward.

Under Cosimo, Florence began to expand its influence outside of central and northern Italy and into the rest of Europe. Though branches of the Medici Bank were located throughout much of Italy and northwestern Europe, it wasn't until Cosimo returned from exile that Florence and the Medici name became almost household words. In 1438, Cosimo managed to convince Pope Eugene IV to change the location for the upcoming council between the pope and the patriarch of the Greek Orthodox Church from the Italian city of Ferrara to Florence. The council was supposed to heal the rift between the two main branches of Christianity at the time, so this move was a great coup for Cosimo and Florence, as it brought not only prestige and renown to Florence but also business. Florence benefited in the short term, but the schism among Christians continued.

Cosimo and the Medici are today remembered mainly for their great patronage of the arts, but at the time, Cosimo, as the de facto power in Florence, had more pressing concerns to deal with than the creations of sometimes ill-tempered geniuses. In addition to running his businesses, Cosimo was faced with important decisions that could decide the future and/or survival of Florence itself.

As we have seen, the Florentines and their allies defeated the greatest threat to their independence, the Duchy of Milan, at the Battle of Anghiari in 1440. As part of the peace that came after the battle, the duke of Milan, Filippo Maria Visconti, had given his daughter in marriage to the mercenary commander of Florence's armies, Francesco Sforza. The duke had also promised that, upon his death, Milan would be ruled by Sforza. However, when he died in 1447, his will contained a surprise. He had reneged on his promise and, worse, made the king of Naples, the powerful Alfonso I of Aragon, the new ruler of Milan. If Alfonso were to rule the Duchy of Milan along with his territories in the south, he would become the most powerful man in Italy, barring (perhaps) the pope.

Cosimo determined that it was in the best interest of Florence to back Sforza, despite the fact that on the duke's death, the people there had declared a republic; Sforza was decidedly anti-republican. Making matters worse, the Venetians, a powerful republic that rivaled Florence in riches and influence but had allied with Florence in the Battle of Anghiari, came out against Florence and Sforza. Worse still, most of the people in Florence were against the war, especially after the Milanese declared a republic.

Cosimo knew that the Milanese republic would not last—the people of Milan and its surrounding territories were not strong enough to hold off an assault by the king of Naples. He also knew that no matter what the status of Florence's relations had been with Venice, the two cities would always be vying with one another for business, not only in Europe but also in the Middle East due to its access to goods from the Far East and India. The only issue that Florence had with Milan was territorial (not commercial), and if Sforza and his family ruled there, they would be powerful Florentine allies. Additionally, Cosimo reached out for aid from a powerful business partner, Charles VII of France.

The war raged between 1448 and 1454, and Francesco Sforza and the Florentines were victorious. In the end, the situation was so bad in Milan (riots, hunger, etc.) that the Milanese opened their gates and offered him the ducal crown. Surprisingly, Sforza's rule, which lasted until his death in 1466, was surprisingly enlightened. He made Milan a city of Renaissance learning and art. He died a popular ruler, and in an on-again, off-again fashion, his descendants ruled Milan until 1535.

Throughout history, various cities, for one reason or another, have risen to prominence over all the others. In the 18th and 19th centuries, Paris and London vied with each other for prominence. In the 20th century, New York became the cultural and economic capital of the world. Some believe that Shanghai may be the city of the 21ˢᵗ century. From the mid-1400s through most of the 1500s, Florence was that place. It became the richest city in Europe and its cultural center. The Renaissance began in Italy, but to be more precise, it began in Florence. And that's in no small part due to the Medici.

Even before Cosimo rose to preeminence in Florence, Cosimo was a great patron of the arts. In actuality, one of the works he commissioned was Donatello's famous *David* (not to be confused with the more famous *David* by Michelangelo). Donatello's *David* was the largest free-standing statue since the classical era of Rome, but it got Cosimo into hot water before his time in exile; it actually might have contributed to it.

Donatello's David in the Museo Nazionale del Bargello, Florence today.
Rufus46, CC BY-SA 3.0 <https://creativecommons.org/licenses/by-sa/3.0>, via Wikimedia Commons https://commons.wikimedia.org/wiki/File:David,_Donatello,_ca._1440,_Bargello_Florenz-02.jpg

Donatello's statue was especially striking for the time. In addition to recreating a lost art form (the large free-standing statue), the artist also portrayed the ancient Jewish king in a much different light than the vast majority of the art of the time. In most works (usually paintings), David was portrayed as a young boy or as an older, world-weary king. In Donatello's work, as you can see, David is an older teenager or young man, and he is, obviously, nude.

Donatello (1386-1466) worked during what historians have called the Early Renaissance, and the resurgence of the nude in sculpture and painting, which would be a prominent feature of later Renaissance art, was only just being experimented with. As you can probably guess, artists of the time struggled both within themselves and with the church and the people over the morality of painting nude figures. After all, this was a time when religious belief was the most important thing in the lives of the vast majority of people.

Donatello's statue was praised for its skill and beauty, but it was also condemned for its nudity and eroticism. By extension, so was the man who funded the artist, Cosimo de' Medici. Though no one is exactly sure when Donatello finished the statue, it is believed to have been commissioned in the 1430s, just when Cosimo found himself in hot water for the design of his palace and violating the sumptuary laws. We do know the statue was placed in the Medici palace in 1469 and that it had likely been there before that time since Donatello died in 1466. Eventually, however, any controversy about the statue must have faded away, for, in 1494, the statue was moved to the courtyard of the Palazzo della Signoria during another Medici family exile. It would later be moved to other very public places until it finally found a home in the Museo Bargello, where it stands today.

Cosimo also commissioned works by now-famous painters Fra Angelico, Lorenzo Ghiberti, and others. His grandson would commission works from the greatest artists of all time.

After the fall of Rome, much of its accumulated learning, culture, and history disappeared. Heaven only knows what was destroyed in the invasions and sacks of Rome that took place in the latter part of the Western Roman Empire. Luckily, in both the Eastern Roman Empire, which was centered in Constantinople, and in the Middle East, where Rome had colonies and where both the dry air and value placed on education saved much ancient learning, many speeches, histories, dramas, and scientific/medical studies survived. In the West, many manuscripts survived the wars by being hidden away in churches and monasteries, which kept them relatively safe from marauders. Those who did raid these holy places were looking for gold and silver, not sheepskin. The Medici were among the great collectors and sellers of ancient manuscripts. The rediscovery of ancient learning was perhaps the biggest catalyst behind the Renaissance, which, after all, means "rebirth." In this case, the "rebirth" was the renewal of classical Roman and Greek ideas.

In 1444, Cosimo founded the first public library in Europe. In it was an original copy of Emperor Justinian's *Pandects*, a collection of Roman laws. There were also manuscripts of Roman Senator Cicero and the historian Tacitus, poems by Virgil and Pliny the Elder, and works by early Renaissance writers, such as Boccaccio, Dante, Petrarch, and more. Amazingly, the library survived another period of Medici exile in the last part of the 1400s, as well as a move to Rome and then a return to Florence, where it stands today.

Cosimo de' Medici died in 1464. He had two sons: Piero and Giovanni. Both seemed destined for short, unhappy lives despite having all that money could buy at the time, including the finest of educations. Piero was sickly from youth, and Giovanni seems to have been the Renaissance version of the "spoiled rich kid." He loved eating, drinking, and womanizing more than the family business that allowed him to do those things. Despite all of this, it seems that Giovanni was Cosimo's favored son.

Giovanni died in 1463, so Cosimo's last year of life was an unhappy one, with one exception. The only bright spot for him was his grandson Lorenzo, who was a lively child and who, as he moved into his early teens, began his education at his grandfather's side. Lorenzo would propel the Medici to even greater heights.

Cosimo's tomb in Florence. The inscription reads, "Here lies buried Cosimo of the Medici by public decree dubbed 'Father of the Fatherland.'" See the bibliography for an interesting article on the meanings hidden and not-so-hidden in the marble.
Andrea del Verrocchio, CC BY-SA 3.0 <http://creativecommons.org/licenses/by-sa/3.0/>, via Wikimedia Commons https://commons.wikimedia.org/wiki/File:San_Lorenzo,_tomba_di_Cosimo_il_Vecchio.JPG

Chapter 4 – Lorenzo il Magnifico (Lorenzo the Magnificent)

Lorenzo de' Medici had the Herculean task of maintaining the Medici fortune and the family's influence at a time when many wanted to bring the family down. For those of you who are fans of American football and boxing, an often-heard comment is that "It's easier to win the championship than keep it." On the way up, there are many contenders, and it's easy to hide among the pack. But once you are at the top, you become a target. Boxers and quarterbacks will tell you that every match or game played as a champion is much more difficult because every contender is striving for the greatest prize—defeating the man, woman, or team at the top. Lorenzo experienced exactly the same thing, but for him and his family, the contest was life and death.

However, before we get to the full life of Lorenzo, we should discuss two other lesser-known members of the Medici family.

Cosimo's illegitimate son, Carlo (1428/30-1492), was sent into the priesthood, although it was not by choice. However, in Florence in the 1400s, one did not generally go against a father's wishes. And being that Carlo's father was who he was, Carlo obeyed rather than face life alone as a "bastard," as it was so ingloriously put at the time. He rose far in the ranks of the Catholic Church, and he became one of the church officers at the cathedral in Florence and an administrator of two nearby churches as well. Additionally, he held the powerful position of tax collector for the papacy, and he was the pope's representative in Tuscany. Like his father, Carlo collected art—in this case, a large collection of medallions, some of which can still be seen in Florence today.

Carlo de' Medici from a painting by Mantegna.
https://commons.wikimedia.org/wiki/File:Ritratto_di_Carlo_de%27_Medici.jpg

More important to Lorenzo's story was his father, Piero. Piero was Cosimo's eldest son, and he was known as "the Gouty" for the sometimes debilitating disease from which he, his father, and his son suffered. When Cosimo passed away, Piero was already forty-eight, which made him almost an old man in the 1400s. However, that meant that Piero had been running the day-to-day operations of the Medici business, with consultation from Cosimo, for quite some time.

Piero was born in 1416, and he was given the finest education that money could buy, though it seemed that he might not live long enough to put it to use. Aside from suffering from gout, he was sickly and relatively weak as a child. However, in a painting that placed the Medici and their allies into the biblical story of the Magi visiting the Christ Child, Piero seems healthily stout, and contemporary statues of him show a man who seems neither sickly nor fat.

Piero in a painting by Gozzoli, 1459-1460, which adorns the walls of the Palazzo Medici.
https://www.wikiart.org/en/benozzo-gozzoli/procession-of-the-magus-balthazar-detail-1461-7

Aside from the "trial" that led to his brief period of exile, Cosimo most likely faced a number of plots since he was both tremendously rich and immensely powerful. However, he must have been successful in either nipping them in the bud or avoiding them. One plot he avoided was led by rival banker Luca Pitti, who had gained the office of Gonfaloniere of Justice. The coup, which took place in 1458, failed, and Pitti was exiled. Pitti eventually returned to Florence after the death of Cosimo, and he seemingly worked hand in hand with Piero in furthering the cause of Florence in both Italy and Europe.

In Piero's case, the plot, like so many in history, came (at least partially) from within. When Cosimo drew up his will, he believed that Piero would need assistance running the Medici empire and named a trusted adviser to help Piero with both the business and political arms of the Medici enterprise. This was Diotisalvi Neroni, who had been with Cosimo for some time and had helped Cosimo return to Florence after his exile.

After two years in power, Piero was faced with challenges from other prominent businessmen and nobles. The adviser Neroni, Luca Pitti, nobleman Agnolo Acciaiolo, and Piero's cousin, Pierfrancesco, developed a plot to kill Piero and topple the House of Medici. This was supposed to happen on August 26th, 1466, while Piero was making the commute from his summer home at the Medici Villa of Careggi outside of the city to his offices in Florence. However, the larger the number of people involved in a plot and the bigger (and richer) the target, the more chance there is for someone to snitch. For years, the Medici had included many leading merchants and guardsmen, among others, on their payroll, which allowed them to get information of all kinds from every level of city life. One of the plotters, a nobleman by the name of Giovanni II Bentivoglio, was either already on the Medici payroll or decided he had more to gain from the Medici than the plotters. Either way, Piero and his son Lorenzo, who was now sixteen and trained in the military arts, were told of the plot.

When the assassins met where they expected Piero and his small guard to be, they were instead met by Lorenzo leading a battalion, which was likely to be between fifty to one hundred men or armed horsemen. The assassins fled, and Piero began his revenge. Firstly, he held an election that was clearly rigged. It moved Medici supporters into positions of power and himself as the absolute master of Florence. Most of the plotters managed to escape, going into lifelong exile, with the exception of Luca Pitti, who threw himself on Piero's mercy. He received it, in a way. Pitti was allowed to return to his home and businesses, but the Medici began a sustained commercial campaign against the Pitti and drove them into bankruptcy within a relatively short time.

Some historians, then and now, argue that the plot against the Medici was actually an attempt to restore Florence to the republicanism it had enjoyed before Cosimo's rise to power. There is an argument to be made here, but considering that Cosimo was exiled for behaving "above his place" and the fact that the plotters were either successful businessmen or nobles, one can't help but wonder if they simply wanted to replace one oligarchy with another.

The plot against Piero's life was not the only challenge that he faced during his brief tenure leading the Medici. One time, the threat came from the Most Serene Republic of Venice (in Italian, *La Serenissima*), Florence's largest commercial competitor. Venice, as has been mentioned earlier, had an immense commercial empire, and it even governed colonies in Greece, the Greek islands, and the Adriatic coast in what is now Croatia and Albania, along with owning trading stations and outposts in North Africa and the Middle East. It also had a powerful navy, which Florence, as a landlocked city, did not (though this would not be a matter of contention when, sometime in the future, Florence gained a port on Italy's western coast).

The leaders of Venice were still stung by what they saw as the betrayal of Cosimo and his support of Sforza, which had led to the loss of Venetian influence in Milan. In 1467, war broke out between the Venetians (led by the famous warrior-mercenary Bartolomeo Colleoni) and troops from the city of Ferrara and other smaller northern Italian cities against Florence, which was joined by Sforza and troops from Milan, the Italian city of Bologna, and troops from King Ferdinand II of Aragon (the man who, along with his wife Isabella of Castile, financed Christopher Columbus's voyages). The short war was won by Florence, which enlarged the city's and the Medicis' influence. (It should be noted, though, that the Venetians were also fighting a ten-year, on-again, off-again war against the rising Ottoman Empire).

In five years, Piero had fought off a plot against his rule and victoriously led (though not on the battlefield himself) Florence to victory against Venice. The effort of running the city and the family business, as well as dealing with the plots and war, took a toll on the already unhealthy and comparatively old Piero, and he died of a cerebral hemorrhage in 1469. While the city offered him a period of mourning, he was not celebrated in death as his father had been. He was also not granted a burial in the Basilica di San Lorenzo as Cosimo had. Still, his tomb was decorated with a statue by the well-known sculptor Verrocchio and was placed in the sacristy of the cathedral, which is still a high honor.

One of Piero's lasting legacies was his patronage of the arts, particularly one artist, Alessandro di Mariano Filipepi. A work by Filipepi is shown directly below.

https://commons.wikimedia.org/wiki/File:Sandro_Botticelli_-_La_nascita_di_Venere_-_Google_Art_Project_-_edited.jpg

Of course, you know this work as *The Birth of Venus* by Sandro Botticelli, which was the name Filipepi adopted in his rise to fame as one of the greatest artists in Europe (and now recognized as one of the great painters of history). Botticelli, like Gozzoli, was also commissioned to paint a "Medici" version of the *Adoration of the Magi*, which included figures from the family, as well as their allies and likely friends in Florence. However, the identity of some of the figures have been lost to time.

In his Adoration of the Magi, Botticelli includes Piero (center, red robe), Cosimo (gifting the Christ child), and Lorenzo and Giuliano, Piero's sons (the foreground at left). It is believed Botticelli included himself as the figure looking at you in the far-right corner. The painting was commissioned by a Medici ally for his tomb, and presumably, he is also in the painting.
https://commons.wikimedia.org/wiki/File:Sandro_Botticelli_-_Adoration_of_the_Magi_-_WGA2702.jpg

When Piero died in 1469, the Medici family business and their power in Florence fell to the eldest of his two sons: Lorenzo. Lorenzo was just twenty years old, which is young by today's standards, but he would have been almost middle age for the Renaissance era. It turned out that he would indeed die a young death (at the age of forty-three), partly from complications arising from gout and poor circulation, just as his father had. But in those twenty-three years as the head of the Medici family, Florence became the center of the European world of culture.

In the late 17th century and throughout the 18th century in Paris, certain liberal nobles, writers, thinkers, painters, and an amazing array of intelligent and talented women formed what had become known as the salon, a place for the intellectuals of the time to discuss the matters of the day, arts, philosophy, politics, and much more. Lorenzo Medici's gatherings in Florence predated the Parisian salons by more than two centuries. Lorenzo's grandfather and father, as well as his educated and politically involved mother, Lucrezia Tornabuoni (her father was from an ancient noble family, and her mother was from an important Florentine family, the Guicciardinis), had provided the best education that money could buy. He learned much of philosophy and politics, not only from his father and grandfather but also from the then-famous Neo-Platonist (a subscriber to the newly rediscovered writings of Plato) Marsilio Ficino. By the time Lorenzo came to lead the Medici, he and his younger brother, Giuliano, were truly at the apex of Florentine society; they had money, intelligence, and good looks (though many would say Lorenzo had a dour and rough edge, despite his apparent good humor on most occasions).

Lorenzo was not called "the Magnificent" by accident. Of course, part of this reputation came from the largesse he showed, not only by commissioning great works of art but also by the amazingly large amounts of money he invested, bestowed, and donated to Florence and its many causes. Perhaps we should stop for a moment and explain exactly how much money we're talking about here.

It's been estimated that the wealth of the Medici at its height, including property, taxes paid, and hard currency (this was the time when meticulous record-keeping and accounting truly began) was, in today's US dollars, an amount approximately that or greater than that of today's richest men: over one hundred twenty *billion* dollars. Lorenzo alone is said to have given (in taxes, donations, civic projects, etc.) nearly half a billion dollars in today's currency. Most of those investments were spent in Florence and its immediate surroundings. So, imagine a city of less than 100,000 (a bit more if we include the surrounding area under its control) in which half a billion dollars were spent in about twenty years. This was the Golden Age of Florence, and Lorenzo was its master for most of it.

Lorenzo knew what being the head of one of Italy's (and Europe's) most powerful families entailed. The bottom line was that there were always going to be many people who were envious, hateful, and/or power-hungry. Competing with the Medici was possible, to a degree, but working with them was a much better alternative. That meant, quite simply, "Either you're for me or you're against me." The other powerful families of Florence (remember, it's not as if the Medici owned the only bank or were the only wool merchants in Florence) felt quite the same way. After all, Renaissance Florence could be a quite dangerous place to play power politics because exile was perhaps the lightest of penalties in a time when dungeons and torture were regularly used.

Lorenzo didn't only know the price of power; he had seen it when the Pitti family had attempted to kill his father. Remember, it was Lorenzo who had chased them off. He would have to face this type of danger in another more effective plot after he came to power.

Lorenzo had learned much from his father and grandfather, but he did make one serious mistake—he forgot that the power of the Medici came from banking and commerce. Any political power they had stemmed from that, not the other way around. Unfortunately, during Lorenzo's twenty-three years as the de facto "lord" of Florence, he concentrated more on politics and less on commerce and banking. Between that and the spending he made out of his passion for the arts and civic feeling, as well as for good living, the Medici fortune began to dwindle. It would be up to his descendants to restore it and the Medici name, but that is still to come.

Even Lorenzo's marriage before the death of Piero was viewed with a political eye. His noble and influential mother traveled to Rome to survey the eligible young women of the upper classes to find a wife for her eldest son. She and Lorenzo settled upon Clarice Orsini, the daughter of an old noble Roman family that claimed descent from the days of the Roman Empire.

Lorenzo de' Medici by Bronzino.
https://commons.wikimedia.org/wiki/File:Lorenzo_de_Medici.jpg

This move was almost purely political, and though Lorenzo did end up loving his wife, he was also notorious for loving other women as well. Still, the marriage united the Medici with an important Roman family and added luster to the Medici name. Not all the Florentines were happy about this marriage for a number of reasons. Among the lower and middle classes, Lorenzo was a popular figure, almost in the same way that an eligible Hollywood bachelor is today, and they wanted to see him married to a Florentine. The upper and upper-middle classes were upset because none of their daughters was considered for the "position" of Lorenzo's wife. However, Lucrezia and Lorenzo knew that if they had chosen among the Florentine families, bad feelings, factionalism, and plotting would invariably follow.

There is another interesting reason many Florentines of the time believed the choice a poor one. Clarice was Roman, and the Roman nobility from which she came was known for its prudishness, strict religiosity, and air of snobbery—all things that most Florentines prided themselves on not being. In actuality, as Florence's influence grew under Lorenzo (and even before), many more conservative Italians looked on the city as a sort of Renaissance "Las Vegas," a "Sin City" in the 15th century.

Lorenzo had a way to calm the feelings of the Florentines: throw a party, or rather, a tournament and a party before the actual wedding. The fact that so many people wrote accounts of the tournament and painted scenes from it over the years means it must have been some party. Lorenzo himself wore the colors of his mother's Florentine family over his armor and won the (non-lethal) jousting tournament. This tournament, which was accompanied by dancing, drinking, eating, music, and games, went on for three full days. Noted Florentine diplomat, author, and friend of the Medici, Luigi Pulgi, wrote a poem in honor of the event (which combined Latin, which was then falling out of use, and Italian, which was gaining in popularity). He also wrote a biography of Lorenzo later in life. It is rumored that Lorenzo aided Pulgi in the formation of the poem, as

Lorenzo himself was quite the poet; hundreds of his quite-skilled poems survive in Florence's museums and libraries today.

Lorenzo's younger brother by four years, Giuliano, might have been even more popular than his elder brother, at least among the ladies and the "playboys" of Renaissance Florence. Whereas Lorenzo wore a dour expression and was likely near-sighted, Giuliano was, by all accounts, the epitome of the handsome Renaissance youth. He was always well-dressed in the bright and fanciful outfits of the rich, and he had shoulder-length curly hair and a classic and handsome Italian face.

Giuliano as seen in a work by Botticelli.
https://commons.wikimedia.org/wiki/File:Giuliano_de%27_Medici_by_Sandro_Botticelli.jpeg

A similar tournament in honor of Giuliano was held in 1475 in one of the large piazzas of Florence. It was there that Giuliano reportedly did such feats on horseback that the famous poet Politian wrote an epic poem in his honor, "The Joust of Giuliano de' Medici," the cover of which is seen below. The event and the poem, which took extreme liberties and created a mythic journey for the wandering knight Giuliano, inspired Botticelli to create perhaps his three greatest works: *The Birth of Venus* (seen above), *Mars and Venus*, and *Primavera* ("Spring").

Primavera by Botticelli. The painting, like his Birth of Venus, created some controversy over its pagan details and semi/full nudity.
https://commons.wikimedia.org/wiki/File:Botticelli-primavera.jpg

On the surface, everything seemed to be coming up roses for Lorenzo and Giuliano, despite the fact that the latter's fiancée died before the planned wedding. One hundred and fifty or so miles away in Rome, a plot against the Medici began.

In 1471, two years after Lorenzo took over from his father, a new pope was elected in Rome. Francesco della Rovere had risen from modest means to the highest position in the Catholic Church at the age of fifty-four and took the name Sixtus IV. As pope, Sixtus was the man responsible for initiating the building of the Sistine Chapel, and he ordered the organization of all Vatican papers and histories into a formal archive, which is still the repository for all church documents today. That's all good, but Sixtus was also responsible for ordering the infamous Spanish Inquisition to begin, which claimed the lives of anywhere between 30,000 to 300,000 people for claims of heresy against church doctrine or other supposed religious crimes (most put the figure somewhere between 50,000 and 100,000). Sixtus was also known for his unabashed nepotism and favoring the causes of his now elevated extended family over anyone else, no matter how qualified they might be.

Sixtus's sister had three children, and the pope pandered to them without shame. One of them, Girolamo Riario, wanted something in particular: to rule Florence. This played into Sixtus's other plans, for he wanted to expand church lands northward from Rome into lands north of Florence that were either allied to, strongly influenced by, or directly controlled by the Florentines (and, therefore, the Medici).

The pope had no compunction in hatching a plot against the Medici with his nephew (and let's be honest, most popes, even to this day, have things they wish *not* to be made public), but in order to do so, he needed help inside Florence. He knew from his clergy in the city that the Pazzi family, which was one of the oldest and still one of the most important families in Florence (one of their ancestors had been second in command to Godfrey of Bouillon, who had taken Jerusalem in the First Crusade) were plotting against him. There was an obvious strain between the families, but Piero the Gouty had married off his daughter Bianca to a member of the Pazzi family, as both families realized that peace was better for business than war. However, with the ascent of Lorenzo and Giuliano, along with their popularity and obvious desire to rule, tensions remained. Within

Florence, it was not unknown for gangs of youths supporting the two families to clash in the streets.

The plotters were very careful about their plans. It wasn't just enough to kill the two leading Medici; they also had to secure Florence and the towns and villages included in the Florentine Republic as well, which they did with armed family members and allies, as well as armed guards on their payroll. Besides the pope, Girolamo Riario, and the Pazzi family, another plotter was the archbishop of Pisa, Francesco Salviati, who had been passed over for the position of archbishop of Florence when Lorenzo gave the "thumbs-down" to his appointment and the "thumbs-up" to the appointment of brother-in-law, Rinaldo Orsini (it's hard to imagine that money and favors did not change hands). Making things even more complicated, the sixteen-year-old Raffaele Riario, who had just been elected cardinal, was due in Pisa to begin his university studies. The youthful cardinal would be accompanied by Archbishop Salviati, and they would pass through Florence on their way to Pisa.

Diplomacy and good relations called for a grand welcome for a visiting archbishop and cardinal of the Catholic Church, no matter how young and inexperienced. This would mean that most of the important families, or at least their leaders, would be invited, including Jacopo de' Pazzi, the head of the Pazzi family. At this banquet, which was held on Holy Saturday, April 25th, 1478, the conspirators planned to poison the Medici brothers and then fill the power vacuum themselves.

Unfortunately for the plotters, Giuliano de' Medici was taken ill, so he did not attend the banquet, forcing them to cancel their plan and come up with a new one. The next day was Easter, and they knew that unless Giuliano was on his deathbed, he would join his brother and the rest of the Medici entourage on the short but crowded journey to the nearby Cathedral of Santa Maria del Fiore. Today, it is known as the Florence Cathedral or the Duomo, and it was the pride of the Medici family and Florence.

The new plan was that at some point on Easter Sunday, when the crowds would be thick in the streets, squares, and churches of Florence, the plotters would attack the two brothers. The opening blow came as Lorenzo and Giuliano were kneeling in prayer in front of their own separate pew. The attackers pounced on Giuliano and fatally stabbed him through the skull with a dagger, then lost their minds in a frenzy and stabbed his lifeless body and head a further nineteen times.

Lorenzo's attacker slashed at his throat and barely grazed the skin. Lorenzo, who, like his unfortunate brother, had been trained in the martial arts, jumped forward, drew his sword, and, along with his friends and bodyguard, fended off the attackers and backed toward the High Altar of the cathedral. They passed through and made their way to the left sacristy (the sacristy is where the clergy's vestments and other holy items are kept) and barricaded themselves in.

The plotters had made serious errors. The first was missing Lorenzo. The second was killing Giuliano in such a savage way. The third and most egregious was trying to assassinate someone in a cathedral on the holiest of all Christian holidays in a time of absolute religious devotion. Within a short time, word had spread throughout Florence about the events at the Duomo. Soon, a mob formed and began hunting down the assassins, who were heading for the main square of Florence, the Piazza della Signoria.

It did not take long for justice to find the plotters. The Gonfaloniere of Justice, a man named Petruzzi, did not know what had happened, but when the archbishop arrived with a group of men, his gestures and demeanor were not in any way normal. Petruzzi brought the archbishop into the Palazzo Vecchio, hiding his suspicions. Once he had them inside, the news of what happened arrived. Within a very short time, the men around Archbishop Salviati were all killed, and the archbishop was strung up and flung over the ramparts of the tower of the Palazzo.

In the meantime, about eighty other people, plotters, and members of the Pazzi family and entourage were killed in the streets. The leader of the family, Jacopo de' Pazzi, escaped to a nearby village, but even then, news of this caliber traveled fast. The villagers dragged him back to Florence upon hearing the news of the violence. Jacopo was soon killed in the Piazza della Signoria. Lorenzo's justice was swift, and the people of Florence, who were angered not only at the idea that their much-loved leader and his popular brother were attacked but also at the method, place, and timing of the attack, supported him. Most of the Pazzi family were killed that day or in the following days. Some were granted exile, never to return to Florence. Lorenzo's sister, the one married to one of the Pazzi, and her son were also sent into exile.

Giuliano's illegitimate son, Giulio, and his mother were welcomed into Lorenzo's family, and the boy was raised as his son. Eventually, he would rise to heights that no one at the time could foresee—he would become Pope Clement VII. For Lorenzo and the Medici, however, times were changing. The assassination marked an end to the banquets and jousts, and Lorenzo, who was beginning to age prematurely, would spend the rest of his short life making sure his descendants were in positions of power that were almost unassailable.

One of the men in the crowd was a certain Leonardo da Vinci, who drew one of the plotters being hanged from the Signoria.
*https://commons.wikimedia.org/wiki/File:Leonardo_da_Vinci_-
_Hanging_of_Bernardo_Baroncelli_1479.jpg*

Before we discuss the massive changes in Florence that were beginning to percolate toward the end of Lorenzo's life, we should remember that it was during his life (and those of his ancestors Giovanni, Cosimo, and Piero) that the Medici slowly took control of the political life of Florence and played a role in both the international politics and business of the time. They were also shaping the culture of Florence by encouraging and commissioning works of art by some of the leading artists of the time, changing the way we look at the world.

Two of the most famous works of the Renaissance era were created in Florence, where they still reside. In virtually any photograph taken of the entire city from the hills around it, the very first thing one notices is the aforementioned Duomo, the first unsupported dome since the time of the ancient Romans. Brunelleschi (1377-1446) was commissioned by Cosimo de' Medici to create the dome for the Cathedral of Santa Maria del Fiore. Cosimo poured millions into seeing the project through.

Brunelleschi had made a name for himself before Cosimo asked him if he could complete the dome of the cathedral. If you are a student of art history, you likely know his name. If you aren't, then you should, for it was Filippo Brunelleschi who developed the first method of using perspective in painting. Giotto (1267-1337), one of those considered to be a forerunner of Renaissance painting, came close to the use of realistic perspective, but even his paintings are flat, using size and height to stress importance and distance, as seen below in his *Lamentation of Christ* (c.1304/5).

Gennadii Saus i Segura, CC BY-SA 4.0 <https://creativecommons.org/licenses/by-sa/4.0>, via Wikimedia Commons https://commons.wikimedia.org/wiki/File:Compianto_sul_Cristo_morto.jpg

The sketches that Brunelleschi did for his architectural and sculptural projects allowed him to illustrate his vision clearly to his patrons, such as Cosimo for the Medici Foundling Hospital, the Basilica di Santo Spirito ("Basilica of the Holy Spirit"), and the church of Santa Maria degli Angeli ("Saint Maria of the Angels"), among many others. It also helped him to see the entire plan exactly the way it was to look before the building or sculpture even began.

There were two problems with Brunelleschi and his dome. Firstly, by all accounts, Brunelleschi was a genius. He also knew it and let everyone else know it. There were more than a few occasions on which he was physically removed from a patron's home after insulting their taste or ideas. Cosimo, however, seemed to have found a match in Brunelleschi or perhaps a polar opposite match, for where Cosimo was generally calm, Brunelleschi was emotional and animated.

The second problem was a Florentine problem. Florence's cathedral was incomplete. It had begun in 1296. Between war, plague, the death of Giotto (who was among the many who worked on it for a time), and much else, the cathedral took eighty-four years to build. And this was without the planned dome, which no one knew how to build in a way that was both economically feasible and structurally reliable.

An incomplete cathedral in a medieval or Renaissance city was a big deal, especially in a city with pretensions such as Florence. The cathedral in medieval Europe was the showpiece of the city, its pride, so an incomplete one was, in many ways, a humiliation. The cathedral in Florence remained incomplete from 1380 until 1436, which was when Brunelleschi and the hundreds of workers and animals finally finished their work.

Brunelleschi's dome would have used more timber to build than was available in all of Tuscany, and the weight of it would have caused it to collapse on itself. The architect decided to build it of brick, which would be supported by even smaller concentric circles of plaster, as well as interlocking stones, bricks, and some wood. Today, it is the largest brick dome in the world and was the first unsupported (meaning beams holding it up from inside the dome) since the Roman era. The machinery to bring up the materials hundreds of feet in the air were also amazing works of technology, and Brunelleschi also had mini-kitchens that hoisted food and drink on scaffolding to his workers so they would not have to take hours to get to the bottom and climb back up, wasting daylight and efficiency.

The interior of the dome today, with paintings by Vasari (1511-1572).
Peter K Burian, CC BY-SA 4.0 <https://creativecommons.org/licenses/by-sa/4.0>, via Wikimedia Commons
https://commons.wikimedia.org/wiki/File:Interior_of_the_dome,_Cathedral,_Florence_(Cattedrale_di_Santa_Maria_del_Fiore).jpg

Michelangelo Buonarroti (1475-1564) is considered one of the greatest artists of all time, if not the greatest, and perhaps the world might not have heard of him if it weren't for the Medici family, specifically Lorenzo, who took young Michelangelo in. He lived in the Medici home for some time as a teenager and was enrolled in the famous Platonic Academy that Cosimo had begun in Florence to spread the philosophical, political, and artistic ideas of ancient Greece and Rome.

Michelangelo, his life, and his works have been written about since perhaps even before his death in the mid-1500s, and he is a secondary character to our story here, but in recognizing the genius of Michelangelo, we must also recognize the genius of those who first saw his talent and allowed it to bloom: the Medici. Michelangelo and a member of the Medici family would famously clash, this time in Rome, when Michelangelo worked on perhaps his most famous works, the ceiling of the Sistine Chapel and his *Last Judgment*.

It shouldn't be forgotten that Leonardo da Vinci's workshop was, for years, located and partially funded by the Medici, primarily Lorenzo. Lorenzo played a key role in securing Leonardo's commission for the duke of Milan, which produced the incredibly famous *Last Supper*.

Diplomacy

When Lorenzo overcame the Pazzi conspirators, his power in Florence and the surrounding countryside was unassailable—at least from within. Even families and people who had been aligned against him saw the assassination attempt as an utterly unacceptable assault on Florentine sovereignty. Worse still was the timing and place of the attack. Despite Florence's reputation as a sort of Renaissance Las Vegas and a center for the learning of pre-Christian philosophy, the city was deeply religious. The Easter Sunday bloodbath in the cathedral offended many and caused them to rally, at least for a time, behind Lorenzo the Magnificent and his family.

Not helping matters, at least for the enemies of Florence and the Medici in the Vatican, were the suspicions that the conspirators had received the blessing of Pope Sixtus IV for their plan. Despite the church's condemnation of the attempt, as well as the plan's timing and setting, many felt that the pope was going to continue his campaign to gain lands for the church in the area surrounding Florence.

Their first clue was the immediate excommunication of Lorenzo, Gonfaloniere of Justice Petruzzi, and the magistrates (legal officers) of the city. Excommunication is defined by Webster's Dictionary as "an ecclesiastical censure depriving a person of the rights of church membership" and "exclusion from fellowship in a group or community" (in this case, the Catholic Church and all Catholics).

Today, excommunication is rarely used, for its meaning and importance have lessened over time. One of those reasons was the split in western and central European Christendom into two main sects: Catholicism and Protestantism. If a Christian was excommunicated from the Catholic Church, odds are they would find their way into another community of Christians with similar beliefs. However, at the time of Lorenzo's excommunication, Catholicism was *the* religious doctrine in Italy and western Europe. There was no other place to go.

More importantly, the Catholic Church (then as now) required the receiving of certain sacraments (such as baptism and the last rites) and the practice of confession (along with penance and the forgiveness of sin by a clergyman) and much else. Without these, the vast majority of Catholics in the Renaissance and most today believe they will not be allowed to spend eternity in the presence of God. That leaves only one alternative: judgment and damnation.

Excommunication had a profound social effect as well. Those who were excommunicated were ostracized; no Catholic was allowed to interact with that individual. Now, of course, this did not happen to Lorenzo and the others in 1478. Most Florentines rallied around the Medici leadership out of anger, loyalty, love, and probably a little dash of economic wisdom. It would be difficult to turn your back on one of the richest men in the world, much less in a city that he ran.

Pope Sixtus did not stop there, though; he forbade any religious service to be held in Florence. That meant that any Florentine who wished to practice their religion would be forced to leave the city and its surrounding possessions, which meant dangerous journeys of days or more in a time of war.

Aside from excommunication, the Vatican had other tools at its disposal. You've already read that the popes of the time had actual armed forces (including, for a time, a navy). Aside from this, the Vatican had access to virtually inexhaustible amounts of money with which to hire mercenaries and entice potential allies. The pope also had the power to name the Holy Roman emperor (and, therefore, give dominion over much of Europe to one degree or another, at least in theory) and to bestow favors (for example, making an illegitimate son a cardinal, etc.).

In this case, the pope cemented his already existing alliance with Ferdinand I of Naples, who was militarily the strongest man in Italy. Sixtus and Ferdinand sought to conquer and divide all of Tuscany (the region in which Florence lies) between them, as well as possibly more of northern Italy in the future.

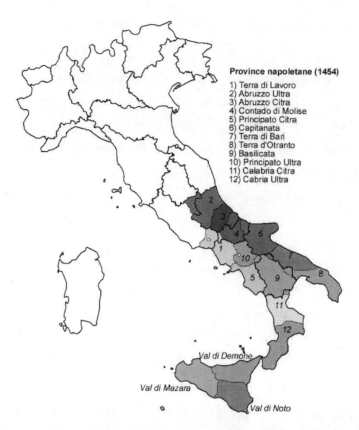

The Kingdom of Naples in 1454. Though large, the central and southern portions of Italy, then as now, were poorer than their northern neighbors.
Wento, CC BY 3.0 <https://creativecommons.org/licenses/by/3.0>, via Wikimedia Commons
https://commons.wikimedia.org/wiki/File:Province_Due_Sicilie_1454.jpg

Ferdinand sent emissaries to the Florentine Signoria, demanding they hand Lorenzo over to the pope to answer for the crime of executing the archbishop. Lorenzo advised the members of the Signoria to agree; he knew that the armies of Florence would not be able to hold out against Ferdinand and the pope for long. Any allies Florence might have normally had were unwilling to help them in this case, even if they wished to. To go directly against the pope risked much more than any reward that might come their way, but the Florentines themselves replied that no matter what happened to them, they would never hand over Lorenzo to Ferdinand.

So, in 1479, a war began, and it did not go Florence's way. The heir to the crown of Naples, Alfonso, defeated the main Florentine force and conducted a campaign of terror and destruction in the countryside. Assaulting Florence itself was both a much more difficult task and probably counterproductive, as much of the physical wealth of the city would likely be destroyed.

Over the course of the year, the Florentines held out, but hardship quickly set in. Despite their protests to the contrary, Lorenzo knew that, eventually, the combination of higher taxes to finance the military (including the hiring of mercenaries) and risking the city and lives for the sake of one man would cause the Florentines to turn Lorenzo over to his enemies.

At the end of 1479, Lorenzo stunned Florence and his enemies, not to mention the whole of Europe after the news had spread, with an unusually brave act. He journeyed alone to see Ferdinand via galley from Pisa to Naples. No guard, weapons, or companions. It was a bold feat, indeed, as Lorenzo's city was at war with this man, a man who had just murdered a famous count at his court after inviting him there as a friend. Not only that, but excommunication meant that, at least in theory, any "good" Catholic could capture Lorenzo and turn him into the pope, probably for a very large reward. Lorenzo would be at the mercy of men who might not hesitate to kill him. Perhaps they would have burned him at the stake after torturing him.

Fortunately for Lorenzo and Florence, that did not happen. When he arrived in Naples, he asked to be taken to Ferdinand, who admired the courage shown by the Florentine and invited him to parley. Cleverly, Lorenzo admitted that Florence was getting weaker but that its resistance would continue if necessary, clearly illustrating how costly the war would be for not only Florence but also him. Lorenzo the Magnificent (the nickname became much more widely used after this episode) pointed out that he knew that Ferdinand's other war with the Ottoman Empire was not going well and that the king was both at risk of going broke and losing his possessions in Dalmatia (the region along the coast of Croatia opposite Italy across the Adriatic) to the Turks. Lorenzo also sowed the seeds of doubt in Ferdinand's mind about the intentions of Pope Sixtus IV, ultimately convincing the king that the pope wished to see northern Italy divided to strengthen his own claims there. Lorenzo told him if that were to happen, the pope would be in a stronger position to renew his claim as sovereign of Naples and force Ferdinand to become the pope's vassal. Worse yet, the Ottoman Turks might cross the Adriatic and conquer a divided Italy. The best situation for both of them, Lorenzo pointed out, was to make peace, and without explicitly saying so, Lorenzo knew he would have to pay Ferdinand a large amount of money to do so.

Lorenzo was kept as a prisoner for three months while Ferdinand mulled over the situation and watched events unfold both in Italy and against the Turks. Luckily for Lorenzo, his confinement was a diplomatic one, and he was treated as an honored guest, dining with the king and his ministers and making friends among them with his wit, knowledge, good manners, and seemingly cheerful attitude. This must have been difficult to keep up; for the first few weeks of his confinement, word kept reaching Naples of Alfonso's continued success against the Florentines. That news was made worse by the pope's incessant demands that Ferdinand turn Lorenzo over to him. A Neapolitan victory over Florence likely meant the end of that city's independence and perhaps the end of the House of Medici. If Lorenzo was turned over to the pope, well, "the stake" was waiting.

By all accounts, Lorenzo's new friendship with the king's minister of state, as well as the respect Ferdinand gained for Lorenzo throughout his confinement and the logic of his arguments, caused the king of Naples to sign a peace treaty with Lorenzo. He gifted Lorenzo a prized stallion and sent him back home on a royal galley. When he arrived in Florence, the city gave him an incredible welcome filled with parades, dinners, and entertainments of all kinds.

Naturally, Pope Sixtus was incensed and threatened to continue the war against Florence on his own, but in the end, the pope's mind was made up by the Turks, who landed a sizable force on the Italian Peninsula in 1480 and threatened to destroy Rome. At that point, Sixtus "miraculously" saw the wisdom of making peace with Lorenzo. "The Magnificent" sent envoys to the Vatican. There, they bowed in submission to the pope, who made peace with the Florentines and revoked the excommunication of its leaders. The price of peace for Florence was to equip fifteen galleys for the pope's navy to battle and repulse the Turks, which was done shortly afterward.

The Golden Age

In 1480, when the war with Naples ended, Lorenzo was thirty-one. He had twelve years left to live. Although he died as a relatively young man, even for that day and age, he led one of the fullest lives one can imagine. Lorenzo himself wrote over one thousand poems, many of which are considered some of the most excellent examples of Renaissance literature. His court was always full, not only with family and friends but also visitors from practically every corner of the known world. And they came to Florence to not only see the city but also meet with its "magnificent" leader. Florence was filled with philosophers, politicians, artists, and musicians. It was the Renaissance version of Paris in the mid-1700s and New York in the 1920s, but it wasn't to last much longer.

While Lorenzo's successful diplomatic approach worked, that success came at a large price: indemnities and bribes paid to Ferdinand and the church, a number of very large bad loans, and incredible expenditures on patronage, civic projects, and much else.

Lorenzo was also conscious of the fact that the Medici men, with the exception of Cosimo the Great, did not live long. He already was afflicted with gout, as his father had, and the stress of his position was clearly aging him. He looked ten years older than he was, and he was going gray in his rapidly receding hairline.

Another source of both stress and expense was Lorenzo's concern with the future of the Medici family. His second son, Giovanni, was made cardinal three years before Lorenzo's death in 1489 at the age of fourteen (again, not an uncommon occurrence at the time), but this and the placement of his brother's son, Giulio, into the clergy cost exorbitant amounts of money in bribes and gifts for those who could make things happen, which included the pope. By the end of his life, Lorenzo had spent, bribed, and loaned the Medici Bank, the source of the family wealth, into a dangerous situation. In the last year or so of his life, the familiar sight of merchants, farmers, and others bringing "gifts" to the Medici offices in search of a meeting with Lorenzo to ask a favor came to an end. People were being turned away, and not only did that signify the end of an era but also change, anger, and weakness.

Savonarola, the Death of Lorenzo, and the First Fall of the Medici

History seems to operate on a pendulum or is caught in an endless circle of action, reaction, and counter-reaction. In Florence, during the last year of Lorenzo's life, a significant portion of the Florentine population was growing tired of Medici rule. Up to this point, our description of Lorenzo's rule in Florence was a Renaissance "era of good feelings," but no one rules by charm and riches alone, no matter how charismatic they are. Governing, especially during the Renaissance era, was exceedingly dangerous, as we have seen. Additionally, once one has power, it is very difficult to give it up; that is why the Roman general Cincinnatus, who could have been the dictator of the early Roman Republic, walked away from power. He was idolized by none other than George Washington, and they are both held up as virtuous icons for giving up their power when they could have had complete power for life.

To keep power, especially during the Renaissance, a man had to be ruthless. While contemporary reports note that Lorenzo did not employ assassins as many other Italian leaders did at the time (this may not be completely accurate), he certainly used intimidation, actual force, and economic and legal warfare to stay in power. Naturally, this bred resentment—and enemies.

Strangely enough, however, despite all of the noble and wealthy families within Florence who wanted to supplant Lorenzo and his family, the Medici were replaced for a time by a Franciscan monk named Girolamo Savonarola. He is also known as Fra Girolamo (for the short form of the Italian word for "brother," *fratello*) or just Savonarola (as he is most often called).

Savonarola by Italian master and brother monk Fra Bartolomeo, c. 1489.
https://commons.wikimedia.org/wiki/File:Girolamo_Savonarola.jpg

Savonarola was born in 1452 in Ferrara, about seventy-five miles northeast of Florence, to a wealthy and academically gifted family. Savonarola's grandfather was a physician, and he was known for berating the elevated personages he served for pursuing romance rather than a more ascetic and healthy life combined with religious practice. Still, his talent, drive, and intelligence were profound, and the family managed to become relatively wealthy within a short time. Savonarola's father, Niccolo, was of middling talent, but his mother was driven, and she encouraged learning and education to her seven children, of whom the future monk was the third.

As a boy and teenager, Savonarola appears to have been much more interested in the workings of the mind rather than the body. He would hide away to learn, not the teachings of the "new" Renaissance thinkers and their opinions on the thoughts of the ancient philosophers, such as Socrates and Plato, but those of more recent times. For him, the religious and spiritual teachings of Saint Augustine and Saint Thomas Aquinas held more value.

Girolamo attended the University of Bologna, which was the oldest true university in Europe, founded in 1088. Think of that for just a moment. Harvard, the oldest university in the United States, was founded in 1636–548 years after the still-functioning institution in Bologna. At Bologna, he proceeded to alienate himself from the rest of the students, who, like students 548 years later, were interested not only in academic studies but also worldly ones.

Some of his many letters home survived. In one of them, it is easy to see that Savonarola was not much different than students who find themselves out of their element when they go out into the wider world. "To be considered a man here, you must defile your mouth with the most filthy, brutal, and tremendous blasphemies...if you study philosophy and the good arts you are considered a dreamer, if you live chastely and modestly, a fool; if you are pious, a hypocrite; if you believe in God, an imbecile." As you might notice, Savonarola in the 1400s sounds much like many of the reactionaries that would follow him up to the present day.

In 1474, Savonarola witnessed a famous monk of the time give a fiery sermon in Ferrara. Many of the city's residents were suddenly swept up in the spirit of religious fervor and regret and began a bonfire, in which they threw jewelry, playing cards (then a relatively new thing), party costumes, and other frivolities. This obviously made an impression on the young man, for not too long afterward, he left home and entered a Dominican monastery against his parent's wishes. At first, he wrote home, asking kindly for forgiveness, but when they wrote back asking him to turn his back on the monastery and become the doctor they wished him to be, he opened upon them in the manner in which he would soon become famous throughout Europe. "Ye Blind," he wrote, "why do you still weep and lament? You hamper me though you should rejoice...what can I say if you grieve yet, save that you are my enemies and foes to Virtue? If so, then I say to you, 'Get ye behind me, all ye who work evil!'" The writing is messianic to the point of quoting Christ.

For six years, Savonarola worshiped and labored in the monastery in Ferrara. During that time, he asked to do nothing but the humblest and "demeaning" of tasks, such as cleaning waste buckets, in the vain hope of learning humility. His ability as a speaker was recognized by the senior monks there, and Savonarola was sent to Florence, which was, at that time, the recognized "den of iniquity," at least to religious Italians. However, within a short time, the monk had bored the Florentines who worshiped at the church of San Lorenzo to tears with his pedagogic style. So, he was given a new job: teaching new monks.

Over the next five years, Savonarola taught the new brothers and lived in a small cell, in which he engaged in what he saw as "spiritual warfare" with Satan and his minions. At the time and surviving until even the early 20th century in some monasteries in Europe, scourging was a popular method of both purging oneself of evil thoughts and showing your devotion. Fra Girolamo frequently whipped himself into a literal lather in order to drive out what he believed was the evil within him.

He also began to adhere to the teachings of the later 12th/early 13th-century Italian monk, Joachim of Flora, a popular teacher who believed that God's final judgment was coming soon and determined that a new age of God was coming. To prepare the people for it, he prescribed a strict and pious life. Joachim of Flora became influential throughout Europe, and monastic orders were founded based on his teachings, but in the end, many of his teachings were condemned as heretical. Since Joachim lived in the time before the Inquisition, he was allowed to live. In the Renaissance era, though, people expounding heretical thoughts, especially after being told not to, might very easily find themselves on a pile of tar-soaked branches.

Why do we digress from discussing the Medici to Savonarola? Simple: despite all of the plotting, assassination attempts, and political maneuvering by the enemies of the Medici inside Florence and out, it was a simple Ferrarese monk who brought the Medici rule in Florence to an end, at least for a time.

By 1490, Lorenzo de' Medici had become one of the most loved people in Europe. His wit, knowledge, and hospitality were legendary. He used his position and esteem to broker diplomatic and financial agreements throughout western Europe. His contributions to the civic life of Florence live today, some five hundred-plus years later.

Of course, one can simultaneously be loved and hated. As we have seen in the assassination attempts on Cosimo, Piero the Gouty, and Lorenzo (and his brother), many people within Florence and without envied and hated the Medici and wanted to replace them. Along with that, a good percentage of the people of Florence wanted a restoration of the republic and some semblance of choice in who ran their city.

Already mentioned were the huge expenditures of Lorenzo, some by necessity, some by choice. Making things more difficult was the fact that the very business that launched the Medici—wool-making and trading—was facing economic challenges. The wool and linen makers of England and northern Europe were growing and expanding at the expense of Florence, which cut into the Medicis' profits and the incomes of many Florentines. In actuality, in the last years of Lorenzo's rule, Florence was experiencing an economic depression.

The people of Florence also knew that those at the top of the economic and social ladder used bribery and other forms of corruption to advance their agendas and frustrate those of their enemies. This could also include "the people" themselves; the wealthy were deathly afraid of another revolt like that of the Ciompi years earlier. Those at the top included not only the Medici and other wealthy families but also many of the clergymen in Florence and the Vatican. In 1490, the Protestant Reformation was just twenty-seven years away, and the rumblings of it were already being felt. They expected it, and they were growing tired of it. Fra Girolamo Savonarola was ready to do something about all of it.

In 1490, Savonarola started preaching again, except this time, he did not use the pulpit as a sort of lectern from which to "teach" his audience. Like demagogues before and after him, Savonarola learned that it is easier to appeal to people's emotions rather than intellect and much easier to reach the negative in people than the positive. He placed himself in the role of an Old Testament prophet. Rather than preach the love espoused by Jesus, he began to condemn not only the lifestyles of many Florentines but also the city itself as a modern-day (for then) version of Sodom and Gomorrah. Chief among his targets were the rich, especially Lorenzo de' Medici.

In today's vernacular, we would call Savonarola a "militant fundamentalist." Though the following comparison is a bit awkward because of the differences in their respective religions, the best way for 21st-century readers (especially those fifty and over) to picture Savonarola is as a "Renaissance Ayatollah Khomeini" (the Islamic fundamentalist who led the Iranian Revolution of 1978/79): severe-looking, joyless, and determined.

Savonarola condemned Florence as a city that had been "de-Christianized." He believed that the only way to save it, both in this world and the next, was to overthrow the existing order and replace it with a theocracy—with himself at its head.

For almost three years, Savonarola preached against the "sin" of Florence and the corruption of its leaders, and his number one target was always Lorenzo. By all accounts, Lorenzo never responded publicly to any of the attacks launched against him by Savonarola. As time went by, Savonarola's influence grew, especially among the poor of the city, and Lorenzo likely knew that any attack against the monk would likely lead to a revolt of one kind or another, given the economic hardships that existed toward the end of his life.

In March 1492, Lorenzo, who found himself increasingly falling ill, had himself carried home to his villa in the village of Careggi, just outside the city. He was accompanied by the philosopher Pico della Mirandola and the poet/scholar Politian, who were both long-time friends who often comforted Lorenzo in times of trouble.

At Lorenzo's request, Savonarola met him and his friends. He heard Lorenzo's deathbed confession and gave the Medici leader absolution and the last rites. Politian included the event in his later memoirs. According to legend, Savonarola asked Lorenzo to issue a deathbed decree that returned Florence to a republic, which he refused to do. With that refusal, Savonarola is reputed to have refused Lorenzo the last rites and absolution, which, according to Catholic belief of the time, would condemn Lorenzo the Magnificent to hell.

This scene was held to be true for centuries, and it was likely put forward by Savonarola's detractors at a later date, for Politian makes no mention of the episode in his memoirs even though he records the death of Lorenzo in much detail. However, something may have happened between them, for we do know that Lorenzo de' Medici spent the last days of his short but glorious life in absolute fear of death. He finally passed on April 8th, 1492, at the age of forty-three.

The death mask of Lorenzo in the Palazzo Pitti, Florence, today.
Possibly Orsino Benintendi, CC BY-SA 4.0 <https://creativecommons.org/licenses/by-sa/4.0>, via Wikimedia Commons
https://commons.wikimedia.org/wiki/File:Lorenzo_death_mask.jpg

When Lorenzo died, his eldest son Piero (known as "the Unfortunate") took over the House of Medici and Florence. Piero was unfortunate in many things, two of which he was not responsible for: the popularity of his father (and the glorious shadow he cast in death as well as life) and his wife, Alfonsina Orsini. She was chosen and negotiated for by Piero's uncle Bernardo, and she was a distant cousin on his mother's side.

As many children of famous parents will tell you, it is often difficult to be judged on your own merits or lack of them—you are always compared to your famous elder. And in this case, Piero's father was one of the most powerful and influential men of the entire Renaissance period. Piero was bound to fall short.

Piero's wife was another problem. Like Piero's mother, she was from outside Florence, which was a bad start already. By all accounts, she was also coarse and unpleasant in an age when courtly manners were highly prized. Later in life, she would both jeopardize the place of the entire Medici family with her behavior and poor manners and help her son, Lorenzo II, rule. And though she did support causes for the poor, she also helped keep her problematic brother-in-law, the controversial Pope Leo X, solvent.

Two years after the death of Lorenzo, Piero was met with a challenge for which he was completely unready. The king of France, Charles VIII, had plans to attack and seize the Kingdom of Naples, which he believed rightfully belonged to him. In order to get his armies there, Charles needed to pass through Florentine territory. Piero refused to grant him permission, fearing that, once in the city, the French would never leave. It was a miscalculation, for Charles did not have designs on Florence, but Piero's refusal to allow his army to pass through left the French king no choice. By the fall of 1494, his army had seized an outlying Florentine fortress and threatened to march on Florence itself. Piero approached Charles with an offer that he hoped would take the French king around Florentine territory, not through it.

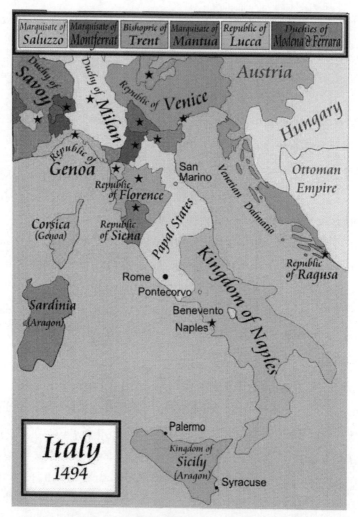

A political map of the Italian Peninsula circa 1494
CC BY-SA 3.0 https://creativecommons.org/licenses/by-sa/3.0/ via Wikimedia Commons
https://commons.wikimedia.org/wiki/File:Italy_1494_AD.png#file

Charles publicly agreed that he would not occupy Florence but refused to take his troops around the city. Additionally, he insisted on taking the Florentine possessions of Pisa and the important port of Livorno, as well as a series of forts that led to Florence itself.

If Piero had anticipated a grand welcome for keeping Florence at peace and unoccupied, he was sorely disappointed. Virtually everyone in the city, from peasants to members of the city government, thought him only one step up from a traitor. By not fighting at all, Florence had lost its honor, and this was made worse by the helpless position that Piero had put the city in with the loss of the fortresses.

The Signoria and virtually every branch of the city government rebelled against Piero and his "primary branch" of the family, which had ruled the city for seventy years. This also included the peasantry and members of the "secondary" branch of the Medici, which was led by two of Piero's cousins.

Piero and his two clergymen brothers were forced to flee Florence. His brother, Giovanni, then a cardinal, had already been forced to flee Rome because he had voted against the eventual winner of the papal election of 1492, Pope Alexander VI (known before his election as Rodrigo Borgia—that other (in)famous Renaissance family, this time from Spain).

The three brothers had fled Florence and were followed closely by a mob. They packed what they could carry as far as cash and jewels and made their way to a series of temporary lodgings in Italy for the next five years. In Florence itself, the Signoria seized large amounts of cash and property from the Medici and the Medici Bank and put a four thousand gold florin bounty on Piero's head.

Piero managed to recruit mercenary armies for three separate attempts to retake the city for his family, but all were miserable failures. In the end, he approached his former enemy, Charles VIII of France, and offered what aid he could in Charles's attempt to seize the Kingdom of Naples in exchange for French help in regaining Florence. As you read, Piero's nickname was "the Unfortunate." While transporting artillery for Charles, Piero's ship sank, and he was never seen again.

His two ecclesiastical brothers, Giovanni and Giuliano, traveled through northwestern Europe, settling for times in France, the Netherlands, and assorted German states.

What of Savonarola? Upon the fall of the Medici, Charles VIII marched his troops into Florence, where he was greeted by Savonarola as a liberator, though Charles imposed tough conditions on Florence (a huge financial penalty and more of its lands, fortresses, and villages). Appeased, Charles marched south, keeping his promise not to occupy or annex Florence itself. When he did this, Florentine history took a strange turn.

Almost immediately, the Florentine families began to turn on each other. It seems it wasn't so much the fact that the Medici ruled Florence but that *they* were not. In the chaos of post-Medici Florence, Savonarola, with the support of a public that had become increasingly radical against the elite and more fanatically religious, took power into his own hands.

For the next five years, Savonarola and two of his fellow monks ruled Florence in all but name. With their rule, many in Florence began to adopt a more ascetic and monkish lifestyle. Some gave away all of their money and wealth. Others changed their mode of dress from the typically colorful and flamboyant way Florentines had dressed for centuries into solemn blacks, whites, and grays. Jewelry was hidden, thrown away, or donated. Gangs of self-appointed morality police roamed the city, chastising women for dressing immodestly and looking for those who had not gotten Savonarola's message and were still risking their (and the city's) soul by gambling and womanizing.

The most infamous event in the five-year reign of Savonarola was the so-called "Bonfire of the Vanities," from which the famous 1987 novel by Tom Wolfe took its name. On February 7th, 1497,

Savonarola began preaching and encouraging the citizens of Florence to denounce their worldly possessions and burn them in the Piazza della Signoria. Hundreds of people, from rich to poor, created a giant bonfire, which burned until late the next morning. In it were jewels, clothing, wigs, cards, gold, musical instruments, novels, and other popular literature and pictures deemed "un-Christian." It has been rumored for years that even Botticelli himself was caught up in the fervor and burned a number of his own paintings that depicted mythical Roman or Greek settings, but this has never been proven conclusively.

However, like so many authoritarians before and after him, Savonarola got carried away. The secular power and influence he had, combined with his unrelenting criticism of the corruption and hypocrisy he saw in the Catholic Church and the papacy, made him enemies in high places. Very high places.

At the end of 1497, the Vatican sent a delegation to the city and demanded they hand Savonarola to them. After a few months of deliberation and maneuvering, the Signoria turned on Savonarola, who was making more enemies within Florence and without by the day with his increasingly severe and personal rule. In April 1498, the Florentines arrested Savonarola and his two accomplices, Brothers Domenico Buonvicini and Silvestro Maruffi, and subjected them to torture. Shortly thereafter, a papal delegation returned to Florence and held a short trial. Savonarola confessed to having made up his visions and prophecies of doom. The three were first excommunicated, then hanged in the same piazza where they had burned the Florentines' possessions. They were then set afire.

Detail of a 16th-century painting of Savonarola and monks being burned in Florence.
https://commons.wikimedia.org/wiki/File:Hanging_and_burning_of_Girolamo_Savonarola_i n_Florence.jpg

Chapter 5 – The First Medici Pope

With both the Medici and Savonarola gone, Florence quickly returned to the infighting it had seen before the rise of the Medici. Again, as they had over a century before, the families of Florence realized that despite all of their individual desires to rule or dominate the city, the best course of action was to stop the fighting and get back to business and some semblance of normalcy.

For that to happen, the Florentines returned to the system similar to one of those we described at the start of this book: they named a lifetime gonfaloniere, who would act like the old podesta, as an outside and impartial man. In this case, it was a man named Piero Soderini, who presided over the fading influence of Florence until 1512, when the Medici returned after eighteen years of exile.

In that time, Giovanni and Giuliano had reconciled with Pope Alexander VI and lodged themselves mainly in Rome. Throughout that time, Giovanni lobbied both Alexander VI (who died in 1503) and Julius II (who took the papal crown following Alexander) to help the Medici return to power in Florence. He argued that stability in

Italy and a renewed and friendly relationship between Florence and the Catholic Church depended on the Medici returning home. In 1512, Ferdinand II of Spain (now ruling Spain and its possessions alone after the death of Isabella) sent troops on behalf of the pope to seize Florence, and with them marched Cardinal Giovanni de' Medici.

In Florence, Gonfaloniere Soderini sought the advice of one of his advisers, a certain Niccolo Machiavelli. You may recognize the name from his famous work, *The Prince*, a handbook for rulers that was dedicated to Lorenzo II, the grandson of Lorenzo il Magnifico, for whom he used to work as a minor diplomat. Machiavelli wrote the work and dedication in 1513, partially to get back in the good graces of the Medici when they returned to power.

However, Machiavelli recommended against supporting his former employers and advised Soderini to hire mercenaries to defend Florence. We tend to think of Machiavelli as this perfect political thinking machine, but in this case, he was very wrong. The mercenaries and Soderini fled due to the threat of the Spanish and papal armies. When they entered the city at the end of August after a terrifying sack of a small nearby city, the Medici returned to power. Incidentally, Machiavelli remained. He denied plotting against the Medici but was tortured and forced into exile, where he remained for the rest of his life.

The family (Giovanni, Giuliano, and their cousin Giulio, along with Piero the Unfortunate's widow Alfonsina and their son Lorenzo) moved back into their palace, but within a short time, Giovanni returned to Rome, handing control of Florence to his brother Giuliano.

The reason for Giovanni's return was the illness and imminent death of Pope Julius II, who had become pope in 1503. Julius died on February 21st, 1513. Julius's accomplishments included the prevention of Italy's domination and, most notably, his patronage of and friendship with Michelangelo. Under Julius, Michelangelo had painted the world-famous ceiling of the Sistine Chapel.

When the College of Cardinals met for their papal conclave (the election of a new pope), they chose Cardinal Giovanni de' Medici, who took the papal name of Leo X. Giovanni was elected over Raffaele Riario, who you might remember from the plot against Lorenzo the Magnificent. Giovanni, who was younger than Riario, had the support of most of the younger cardinals and those who came from noble families, which almost ensured a victory before the election was held.

As you have read, it was not unusual for a boy in his teens to be placed into the College of Cardinals. Part of the reason was that, at the time, a cardinal did not have to be ordained as a priest. As a matter of fact, Giovanni held the position while only maintaining the clerical rank of deacon. Before he was given "the Keys to the Kingdom," Giovanni was first ordained as a priest and, immediately afterward, consecrated as a bishop, then made pope. He was the last man to hold the office of pope who had not been a priest first.

Raphael's Portrait of Leo X, c. 1518-1520. (L) Giulio de' Medici, the future Pope Clement VII, and (r) Medici cousin Luigi de' Rossi.
https://commons.wikimedia.org/wiki/File:Portrait_of_Pope_Leo_X_and_his_cousins,_cardinals_Giulio_de%27_Medici_and_Luigi_de%27_Rossi_(by_Raphael).jpg

When Giovanni became Leo X, he was under no illusions as to the nature of the papacy in the early 1500s. Though it came with all of the trappings of holiness and the Catholic faith, the position of pope was much more political and worldly than it is today. Leo was determined to use his position as Christ's representative on Earth to increase the power and influence of his family, not only in Florence but also in Italy and Europe.

Leo had been maneuvering for the position for some time, and when he was given the crown of Saint Peter in 1513, he had already loosely determined the course of action he would take when he had the power to do so.

By the time Leo became pope, his nephew, Lorenzo (full name Lorenzo di Piero de' Medici but most often known as Lorenzo II), was in complete control of Florence. Leo's younger brother Giuliano would move on from Florence to bigger and better things, namely control of central Italy under the patronage of his brother, the pope.

Misfortune derailed Leo's plans twice. Giuliano died early like many of the Medici men; he was only thirty-seven. Leo then decided that his nephew Lorenzo would be the secular face of the Medici family, although there was a problem with that: Lorenzo II had none of the skill or talent of his famous ancestor, Lorenzo il Magnifico.

Despite Machiavelli's famous dedication in *The Prince* to him, Lorenzo had no real talent for ruling or leading. He led a life of excess and, more importantly, led the already fading (in influence) city of Florence into a costly war. This war, the War of Urbino, was an attempt by both Lorenzo II and Leo to expand Medici and Florentine influence in central Italy.

Lorenzo wanted to prove his martial talents, of which he bragged but with which he had no experience, by annexing the city of Urbino, which is about seventy miles east of Florence. Urbino was ruled by Francesco Maria della Rovere, whose powerful family had also bred a pope: the previously mentioned Sixtus IV.

It will give you some idea of the nature of politics and power in Renaissance Italy to know that, while in exile, Pope Leo's brother Giuliano (and his wife and son, Lorenzo) had been given refuge for some time with the Della Rovere family in Urbino, specifically the duke of Urbino, Francesco Maria, whom the pope and Lorenzo II now wanted to war on. They had been prevented from doing so by Giuliano, but with Giuliano's death, the way was open for the Medici conquest of Urbino, with the vision of creating an even bigger Medici "empire" in the near future.

On May 30th, 1516, the pope's armies marched on Urbino and ousted della Rovere. Lorenzo was named the duke of Urbino. In the following months, della Rovere hired and used a mercenary army of some five thousand men to try to recapture his city. At some point during the campaign, Lorenzo visited a battlefield for the first (and last) time. He received a head wound, which turned him off combat for the rest of his short life, despite having bragged about his warrior skill beforehand.

Now a man of prestige, with lands, a title, and an uncle as pope, instead of living as an exile, Lorenzo II married into a noble French family with ties to the French king, Francis I. The product of the marriage between Lorenzo and Madeleine de La Tour d'Auvergne was Catherine de' Medici (b. 1519), who was one of the most powerful women in French history. Unfortunately, Madeleine died shortly after giving birth. Lorenzo died of tuberculosis six days later. Ultimately, a deal was reached with Pope Leo X in which the Della Rovere family would return to govern Urbino as part of the Papal States.

The war with Urbino cost both Leo and Florence a significant amount of money, in both treasure and taxes. The people of Florence, who had not exactly been ecstatic about the return of the Medici, began to hate them. For a brief period, Giulio Medici returned to Florence and managed to restore some faith in the Medici rule by lowering taxes, restructuring loans, and returning some republican power to the people of the city. Some years later, as Pope Clement VII, Giulio would again see the Medici fortunes and popularity in Florence decrease. The family would again be exiled from the city but only for a comparatively short time.

In 1529/30, the war between the Republic of Florence and Charles V, the Habsburg emperor (who was also the king of Spain and archduke of Austria), and Pope Clement VII (Giulio Medici) resulted in a Medici victory. At this point, all pretenses of the Medici fully restoring the Republic of Florence vanished. With little interruption, one or another branch of the Medici family ruled the city and/or all of Tuscany as the dukes of Tuscany until 1737. Some of them, such as Cosimo I, who ruled Florence from 1537 to 1569 and then Tuscany from 1569 to 1574, made a name for themselves on the European political stage, and many of them continued the Medici tradition of being patrons of the arts. However, the true "Golden Age of Florence" had passed, and the power of both Florence and Italy slowly began to wane in favor of larger and more united entities such as Spain, France, and England.

Even when Leo X was the pope, the waning influence of Florence and the increasingly authoritarian rule of the Medici could be seen. Since Leo X was in charge of the papacy, he was one of the most powerful and influential men on the planet at that time.

Though the power of the papacy had been waning since the late 13th century and the failure of the Ninth (and last) Crusade, which set out to recapture the Holy Land for Western Christendom (meaning the Catholic Church), the pope was still an immensely powerful and wealthy figure. The church collected taxes all over Europe, much of which made its way to the Vatican. This means Leo X had access to not only his personal wealth and that of the Medici but also that of the Catholic Church. That kind of money can buy a person an awful lot of power.

Of course, just being the pope gave one extraordinary power. In a time when the idea of the divine right of kings (the notion that anyone who became king was somehow blessed by God and put in that position through divine will and, therefore, must be obeyed) was truly beginning to spread throughout Europe. The pope enjoyed not only the idea of divine right but also the idea that the pope was the actual representative of Christ on Earth. He was anointed in an unbroken chain from the disciple (and saint in the Catholic faith) Peter, to whom Jesus said, "And I say also unto thee, that thou art Peter, and upon this rock I will build my church; and the gates of hell shall not prevail against it." (Matthew 16:18, King James Version. The name "Peter" literally means "rock.") That lineage, communicated by God through the choice of the College of Cardinals, meant that the pope was infallible and incapable of error, at least in theory.

Of course, popes and kings/emperors had been struggling with each other for earthly power for centuries before Leo X, and they would do so for centuries afterward. But for most people in Europe and many monarchs, the pope's wish was their command. As we have seen, the pope could wield the ultimate in religious power, that of excommunication—forbidding someone from receiving holy rites (and therefore consigning them to hell) and forbidding any Catholic from associating with them. In the time before the Protestant Reformation, this was a threat that the majority of people took quite seriously. Not only did the popes of this time wield real power on Earth in the form of armies and the Inquisition, but they also held power over an individual's afterlife as well.

We all know the saying, "Absolute power corrupts absolutely." If anyone in 1513 had absolute power, it was Leo X of the House of Medici. Though Leo was, like many of his ancestors, a great patron of the arts, he was also a lover of the good things in life, particularly food and drink but also hunting, gambling, and perhaps homosexual relations (academic opinion is divided on this). We do know that Leo held banquets and receptions for his supporters and international guests at the Vatican. These were lavish in the extreme and could go on for days. It is clear, at least in Raphael's painting above, that Leo enjoyed a good feast.

Despite this extravagance, one of the issues that the church was facing was declining revenue. This happened for a number of reasons.

One reason was taxes. Generally speaking, the people of western and central Europe paid two sets of taxes: one set to their secular rulers and their representatives and another set to the church in the form of tithes, donations, and land taxes. The money paid to the church was both voluntary and involuntary. The Catholic Church in France, for example, was the largest landholder in the country, and while much of that land held churches, cathedrals, monasteries, and convents, a considerable part was rented out to farmers and nobles who had to pay taxes to the church over and above their rents.

Then, of course, were the collections that took place in every place of worship; before the Reformation, those were exclusively Catholic. From the smallest village church to the largest urban cathedral, services were held (and attended) on more than just Sundays and holidays (and many more were celebrated then than now). Considering the number of small churches throughout western Europe, the amount of money coming in added up considerably. Those at the bottom were pressured by both their peers and the local clergy to give. At the top, the nobles and growing middle classes gave, often ostentatiously, to show their "reverence" for the church. Prayers for the dead, masses, and other church celebrations could also cost money.

Add to that the fact that many archbishops and cardinals also played a secular role, especially in the lands that now make up Germany and the former Austro-Hungarian Empire. Entire states were governed by archbishops, many of whom were both rich from birth and from their church offices.

Of course, much of the money collected in churches was not expected to make it all the way to the Vatican. There were local expenses, and up and down the economic food chain, Catholic clergymen took "their cut." The further up the food chain one was, the more they took, and, of course, the pope was at the top.

Leo X loved a good time, as you read above. Like many popes before him, he loved jewels and gold. Leo also happened to love exotic animals, and he kept a menagerie at the Vatican, which included a white elephant. He spent much money collecting exotic animals and also had many "donated" to him by people seeking favors.

While Leo and the Vatican itself collected much money and other valuables in donations, rents, bribes, and gifts, they also spent a lot. Leo's vices have been recited above, but these expenditures also came in the form of financing wars (both his and those of his allies), diplomatic bribes, gifts to kings and other important personages, the building of churches, and the missions to the Americas, which had begun shortly after Columbus voyaged to the Western Hemisphere, as well as those to Asia. Church-sponsored and church-run colleges and universities were being built throughout Europe and would expand around the world. The list of expenditures goes on and on. And don't forget the great cost of running the Vatican itself, as well as the slowly growing competition for both money and power coming from secular kings and queens.

In short, Leo's Catholic Church was hemorrhaging money. It doesn't seem possible after what you just read, but it was, and Leo had to do something about it. Unfortunately for Leo and the Catholic Church, what he did was the wrong thing at the wrong time.

The "wrong thing" was the selling of indulgences. An indulgence, a word whose Latin root *indulgeo* means to be kind or tender, originally meant a favor, but in Roman law, it also came to mean forgiveness of monetary debt and/or taxes. It could also mean a release from captivity. Indulgences were not introduced by Leo X; they had been issued or granted to people for doing particular good works or saying a specific number of prayers for a person or a cause for hundreds of years. In Catholic doctrine, believers whose lives had been generally good and who had kept their faith despite falling to the temptation of certain sins at times would likely be required (by God) to spend a certain amount of time in purgatory to further remove the stain of sin from their souls before entering the Kingdom of Heaven. The basis for the belief in purgatory is rooted in the Old Testament, specifically the Second Book of Maccabees. Casting about for a way to make a lot of money quickly, Pope Leo X and his advisers landed on a new use for indulgences and a new method for issuing them. Indulgences for the removal of sins would be sold to reduce the amount of time one spent in purgatory. Official Vatican indulgences would be sent out to all of the clergy and important churches to be sold throughout Catholic Europe. Local priests and monks would go about with a scribe selling indulgences to reduce one's time in purgatory by a few days (which would be cheap) or by years or maybe centuries (which would be expensive). Additionally, some of the more expensive indulgences would grant the recipient an immediate entry into heaven.

Remember, this was at a time when the vast majority of Europeans were poor and uneducated, but the upper and middle classes bought indulgences too. Though belief in the pope as infallible and as Christ's true representative on Earth was beginning to fade, most people in Europe still believed it. And even if they had doubts, what harm could it do to "play it safe" and buy an indulgence?

Throughout Catholic Europe, Leo's priests and monks sold his indulgences. Of course, real priests sold fake indulgences and pocketed the money. On top of that, throughout Europe, men posed as priests and monks and pocketed the sale of their own fake papal indulgences.

Whether Leo actually believed in the power of indulgences is doubtful. It did not matter as long as it brought in money, and it did—lots of it.

As you can probably imagine, this corruption did not go unnoticed, even by those who bought indulgences. The church already had a number of ways of expiating sin, including confession and penance. Some clergy were able to do exactly what the flimsy pieces of paper being sold were doing, although they granted indulgences and did not sell them. Now that indulgences were being sold, whose time in purgatory would be lessened and/or who was sent to heaven directly more often than others? The rich. Of course, this bred more resentment.

The feelings of bitterness toward the church and its officials had been growing for some time. The opulence of the Vatican and the lavish life of its officials had been noted and resented for centuries by the time of Leo X. The only clergymen who might actually be truly respected were the small town and village priests, who many times lived in utter poverty like their parishioners.

Some priests in big cities and the majority of bishops, archbishops, and cardinals seemed to love "the good life" a bit too much. Celibacy had been required of the clergy, monks, and nuns since the 10th century, but this was rarely followed for quite some time. Before this,

Catholic holy men could marry and have children. This tradition died hard, and at the time of Leo, it was not unknown for a pope to have had children, to have been or be (secretly) married, or have a mistress or mistresses; this went for bishops and archbishops as well.

Some of the most salacious tales of the Middle Ages and the Renaissance involve monks and nuns. Homosexuality was reportedly rather common, but in a time when homosexuality was both a sin and a perceived threat to the public good, it was frequently overlooked when it came to the Catholic Church. Naturally, the hypocrisy of both heterosexual and homosexual activities in the church bred resentment among the people, as did the rich homes, robes, jewels, and servants of the higher church officials. Some of those jewels, which had been housed in the Vatican for hundreds of years, were sold for cash by Leo's cousin Giulio, the future Clement VII.

Before you get the idea that all of the money brought in by the sale of indulgences went right into the pockets of the pope and his immediate circle, you should know that the "straw that broke the camel's back" regarding many people's tolerance of the church was Leo's expenditures on the reconstruction and remodeling of the Vatican and a number of colleges in and around Rome. Still, much money did find its way into "holy" pockets, and perhaps even more importantly was the idea that the church was allowing and encouraging people to buy their way out of sin and into heaven.

One of the people upset by the events in the Catholic Church was a German priest and scholar named Martin Luther. He had been ordained in 1507 at the age of twenty-four and had visited Rome in 1510. On his visit, he was shocked by the corruption he witnessed, not only in and around the Holy City but also within the clergy.

While in the city, Luther set about climbing the "Holy Stairs" (*Scala Sancta* in Latin), which were said to have been brought from Jerusalem in the 4th century. They were reputed to be the same stairs that led to the hall of Pontius Pilate and on which Jesus had stoodwhile waiting for his trial. At the time, the church told believers that if one climbed and stopped on each of the twenty-eight stairs and said the Lord's Prayer, they would release someone from purgatory. This was an indulgence, but at least one had to perform an act of penance for it. Either way, Luther reported hearing the voice of God over and over again as he climbed the stairs telling him, "The just shall live by faith!" The foundational belief of Protestantism is that man shall be redeemed by faith rather than by good works, and it stems from this moment and by Paul's Letter to the Ephesians 2:8-10: "For by grace you have been saved through faith. And this is not your own doing; it is the gift of God, not a result of works, so that no one may boast."

In 1517, Luther posted what has become known as his *Ninety-five Theses* or *Disputation on the Power and Efficacy of Indulgences*, in which he criticized both the practice of selling indulgences, indulgences themselves, and the corruption of those selling them, which indirectly meant the pope.

Of course, you may recognize the beginning of the Protestant Reformation and the splitting of Western Christendom into two main branches. With this split came great changes in European society; it was a split not only along religious lines but also along geographic lines. Most of southwestern Europe remained Catholic, and most of northwestern Europe became one type of Protestant or another (Luther's belief system split into many sects as well: Lutheran, Presbyterian, Anglican/Episcopal, Calvinist, etc.). Exceedingly bloody religious wars and persecutions began, which continued into the early 1800s.

Though, of course, Leo X was not solely responsible for the Protestant Reformation, his actions finally put the great change into motion, which radically changed the world and the course of history.

Leo X died in 1521, four years after the beginning of the Protestant Reformation, which he had tried unsuccessfully to stamp out. On top of all of the expenditures mentioned above, the wars of the early Reformation cost the papacy what would amount to tens of millions of dollars or more today. This forced Leo's successors to rein in expenses, which only weakened the papacy further. Leo's immediate successor, his cousin Giulio, was actually run out of the Vatican for some time by the army of Charles, Duke of Bourbon, and the German knight Georg von Frundsberg, whose troops ravaged Rome itself while holding the pope prisoner.

Chapter 6 – The Last Great Medici: Catherine

Though the Medici continued to rule in Florence as the dukes of Tuscany and continued their great legacy of being patrons of the arts, their influence steadily waned both in Europe and Italy. In 1737, the great powers of Europe decided to settle a myriad of political questions, one of which involved the handing over of Tuscany and Florence to King Charles III of Spain after the death of Gian Gastone, the last Medici duke of Tuscany. By this time, Tuscany and Florence had grown so weak and poor, despite Gian Gastone's rather welcome and enlightened economic policies, that the duke was not even consulted. Upon the death of Gian Gastone, Tuscany and Florence left the Medici behind.

However, two centuries before that happened, a Medici woman became the power behind the throne in France and presided over some of the most radical changes and events in that kingdom. We have introduced her to you in passing earlier: Catherine de' Medici, daughter of Lorenzo II and Madeleine de La Tour d'Auvergne.

Madeleine was from a powerful aristocratic family from the Auvergne region of south-central France.

Catherine was born in Florence in 1519 during the reign of her uncle, Pope Clement VII. As you have read, the fortunes of the Medici had taken a strange turn from banking and wool-making to holding the high office of pope. However, they had to preside over the beginning stages of the Protestant Reformation and the incredible bloodshed that resulted from it.

Catherine was orphaned by the time she was six days old, with her mother dying shortly after childbirth and her father succumbing to tuberculosis. She was raised mostly in convents at the instruction of the head of the family, her uncle, the pope. He had every intention of keeping her from power. After all, she was the heir of Lorenzo the Magnificent (remember, Clement/Giulio was the son of Giuliano, who had been assassinated in the Florence Cathedral).

Fortunately for Catherine, life in a convent was not as one might picture it. Neither she nor her family intended her for the sisterhood, and like many upper-class girls and young women of the time, she received a thorough Renaissance education. Being a member of one of the most prestigious families in Europe also helped her gain experience. She was not confined to the convent as a novitiate would be, and she frequently attended state dinners and other functions, as well as visited the studios of leading artists and the salons of many of the great thinkers of the time. Additionally, she was raised both in Florence and in Rome, giving her a wide range of experiences and contacts.

Naturally, as a young woman of an important family, Catherine's uncle and relatives were on the lookout for her future husband, who undoubtedly would come from the higher levels of society. Since she was also French by her mother, her range of potential suitors included the French nobility. In 1533, she married the second son of King Francis I of France, Henry of Orleans (who you may know from the story of Henry VIII of England—they were famous rivals). Her wedding was presided over by the pope and attended by the entire royal family of France. Catherine was fourteen at the time of her marriage, which was not unusual at the time and for quite some time afterward. In a time when life expectancy was short, a woman (especially in a noble family) was expected to start a family almost immediately after marriage—the clock was literally ticking. You must also remember that as the wife of a prince, she was expected to behave like an adult and carried serious responsibilities on her shoulders.

Her father-in-law, the king of France, loved her. She was pretty, exceedingly intelligent, cultured, and lively. She loved conversation, dancing, and the arts, as well as the "less lady-like" skills of hunting and riding, at which she was both quite accomplished. As her father-in-law became more and more fond of her, her husband became less. It seems that Henry was actually jealous of her abilities and the place she held in his father's heart. Their relationship was soon strained; it remained cordial, but it was not loving.

Francis I's eldest son (also named Francis) died in 1536 at the age of eighteen, and it was suspected that he died from poisoning. His death was obviously early, and at the time, whenever a royal died at a young age, poisoning was always considered. However, during his brief life, the younger Francis had spent time as a hostage in Spain due to a dispute between that country and France. His captivity was rough, and he spent three years in a cold, dark cell, which many believed cost him his health; he may have contracted tuberculosis there. Still, his personal secretary, who was an Italian by the name of Count Montecuccoli and who had been placed in the position at the request of Catherine de' Medici, had his quarters searched. A book on poisons was discovered. In addition, Catherine herself was known for having an interest in poison and also for the occult, and she was immediately suspected by many of murdering the prince herself. Montecuccoli was tortured and confessed to the murder, but before his execution, he recanted. He was still executed by quartering, in which the victim is tied to four horses by the arms and legs. They are then spurred to run, pulling the arms and legs of the victim apart.

Francis I never seemed to have put any stock in the idea that Catherine poisoned his son. She remained a favorite, but suspicion hung over her for her whole life. Since that time, a variety of writers, historians, and medical historians have concluded that Francis was likely a victim of pleurisy (the filling of the lungs with fluid due to a weak heart) or tuberculosis.

Meanwhile, another woman named Diane de Poitiers, who was twenty years older than the young prince, had captured Henry's heart and attempted to convince the king to grant Henry a divorce from "the Italian," as many people called Catherine behind her back. She stated that Catherine was sterile and unable to provide heirs. Francis refused and instructed his son to start a family. Catherine was indeed very fertile, and she bore *ten* children. Three of these would die in infancy. Four daughters would marry kings, and her three surviving sons would each become king of France.

When Francis I died in 1547, Henry became Henry II, and Catherine's life became difficult. Henry's lover was moved into the royal apartments on his command, and Catherine was pushed to the side and forced to live in seclusion in the castle of Chaumont for twelve long years. There, she is reputed to have not only further developed her intellect but also learned how to hide her true feelings and intentions. Later in life, diplomats and others who came into contact with her would describe her as having "extraordinary self-control," though many of her enemies accused her of being "masculine" and "ice-cold."

For the twelve years of her seclusion, Catherine concentrated on raising her children and on informing herself on world affairs. In 1557, France was at war with the Duchy of Savoy in northern Italy, and the war was not going well. While her husband was away, panic spread in Paris. Catherine went to the Parlement (an advisory body to the king with some power of the purse) and convinced them to raise a large sum of money for the defense of Paris and France. Her appeal was reputedly so effective that it reduced some members to patriotic tears. Eventually, France and Savoy negotiated a peace that was detrimental to neither, as France had been able to hold its own after Catherine's appeal. From that time onward, Henry II treated his wife with renewed respect.

Catherine de' Medici in the 1550s.
https://commons.wikimedia.org/wiki/File:KatharinavonMedici.jpg

In 1558, Henry II was killed in a tournament. A lance penetrated his helmet, entered his eye, and, after ten days of excruciating pain, the king died. Catherine was a widow at forty, and her son Francis now became Francis II, King of France, at the age of fourteen. The duke of Guise, who was the uncle of the famous Mary, Queen of Scots (who was married to the young king), was named regent for Francis. This only brought France deeper into the religious wars going on within Europe and in the country. Francis II, however, died in late 1560; he had only been the king of France for seventeen months. When he passed, his younger brother Charles, who was only ten, became King Charles IX. Catherine decided to take the power of the regency unto herself. Her first act was to end the religious warfare going on in France that was tearing the country apart. She also gave the Huguenots (French Protestants) the right to worship openly and released many from prison. Of course, her enemies accused her of secretly being Protestant, which was not true. And when she came down on the side of Catholics in disputes, the Protestants accused her of being a fanatical Catholic. This probably means she kept a balance between the two.

In 1562, open warfare broke out again in France after the publication of a royal edict, which was written by Catherine in the name of the king. It formally recognized the Protestant religion. That was too much for many, including the previously ousted duke of Guise, who took Catherine and the king prisoner. Civil war spread all over the country, and the English under Queen Elizabeth I landed in two coastal cities, ostensibly to help the Protestants there.

In February 1563, a French knight who had converted to Protestantism shot and killed the duke of Guise. Catherine, who did not have a role in the assassination, nevertheless was not sad about it, and she took power into her own hands again. She brought the warring factions together and forced peace upon them. Simultaneously, she raised a personal army, which marched to the coast and (unexpectedly) defeated the English, driving them back across the English Channel.

Catherine was skilled, but perhaps no one on the planet at that point in time would have been able to end the warfare in France between the Catholics and Huguenots, which broke out into open warfare again in 1567. Another peace was brokered by Catherine. Many diplomats believed her to be an absolute professional in terms of diplomacy and foreign relations, but the peace lasted only until 1568, as other nations became involved in France's internal religious civil wars.

For two years, extraordinarily violent and savage religious warfare continued in France until, once again, Catherine de' Medici came up with a solution. When her son Charles became king, she had married off her reputedly stunning daughter Margaret to Henry of Navarre (a semi-independent kingdom on the border of France and Spain). She hoped that the marriage of her Catholic daughter to the Protestant Henry might serve as an example of the peace that could exist between Catholics and Protestants if given the opportunity.

It did not. On the morning of August 24th, 1572, the radical Catholics of Paris, following the duke of Guise's instructions, began one of the most infamous episodes of French history: the St. Bartholomew's Day massacre. On this day, perhaps thousands of Huguenots were butchered in the streets of the capital. In the days afterward, Protestants began to blame Catherine for the massacre, believing that she had staged the wedding in order to bring as many Huguenot supporters of Henry of Navarre to the city. The duke of Guise was quick to point at Catherine as well, though he was the one to blame for the terrible events.

For the rest of Catherine's life, she attempted to broker peace between the two factions. In the Agreement of La Rochelle, both sides agreed to put down their arms and work toward a peaceful solution. The Protestants, being the minority in the country, were concerned with having sanctuary cities where they would be the majority. This peace lasted five years until bloodshed broke out yet again.

By this time, Charles IX had died, and Catherine's youngest and most favored son, now Henry III of France, took the throne of France. One of his first actions was ordering the assassination of the duke of Guise in December 1588, for, by this point, the Guise family had not only worked against peace in the country but had also attempted to overthrow the royal family and put themselves in their place.

Catherine received the news from her son while she was in bed. She was seventy, although she felt older than her years from her efforts. She believed she was about to die, and she did on January 5th, 1589. She was the last of the senior branch (Cosimo's branch) of the Medici.

France continued to see religious violence on and off for many years until Catholic King Louis XIV ordered the expulsion or forcible conversion of all French Protestants in 1685. To this day, France is an overwhelmingly Catholic country, though tolerance for other faiths has become one of the pillars on which its republic is built.

Conclusion

It's fitting that we end this short history of the Medici family on a high note. While Catherine de' Medici failed to reconcile the Catholics and the Protestants of France, dooming the country to another century of religious strife, her attempts to make peace were more than worthy of the reputation that her ancestors Cosimo the Great and Lorenzo the Magnificent had established in the 1400s.

Either directly or indirectly, the Medici influenced events in Europe and the world from the early 1400s until the late 1500s and beyond. Many historians have drawn the conclusion that the Medici, along with the large Venetian trading companies of the time, helped set the precedent that led to the English East India Company. Some have even likened the Medici to the Mafia, as they both doled out favors to their family members and allies, formed alliances through favors or intimidation, and propelled themselves into the ranks of the rich by the use of artistic patronage. The American public broadcasting station **PBS** (Public Broadcasting Service) makes this clear from the start of its documentary, *The Medici: Godfathers of the Renaissance*, and in many ways, they were.

Today, however, when people think of the Medici family, they think of their patronage of the arts, which very well might be unparalleled in history. Millions of tourists from all over the world (fifteen million in 2019) come to the city that the Medici built to visit the Uffizi Gallery and the Museo Bargello, among other Florentine collections, to see for themselves the beautiful works that the Medici and others sponsored during the "rebirth," or the "Renaissance."

We hope that you have enjoyed Captivating History's account of the Medici family of Florence. With the passage of time, this incredibly influential family has begun to fade from the collective memory, but we should never forget that behind the making of money, political machinations, and violence, the Medici were, in large part, responsible for the amazing period of human history that delineated the line between the Dark Ages and the Renaissance.

Here's another book by Captivating History that you might like

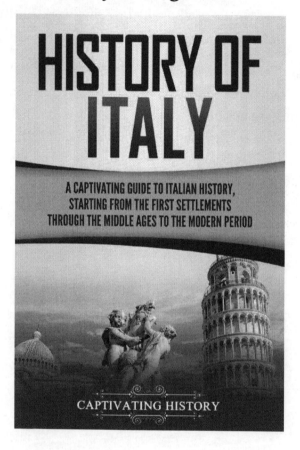

Free Bonus from Captivating History (Available for a Limited time)

Hi History Lovers!

Now you have a chance to join our exclusive history list so you can get your first history ebook for free as well as discounts and a potential to get more history books for free! Simply visit the link below to join.

Captivatinghistory.com/ebook

Also, make sure to follow us on Facebook, Twitter and Youtube by searching for Captivating History.

Bibliography

Brucker, G. RENAISSANCE FLORENCE. University of California Press, 1983.

Burckhardt, J. THE CIVILIZATION OF THE RENAISSANCE IN ITALY. Simon & Schuster, 2013.

Cesati, F. THE MEDICI: STORY OF A EUROPEAN DYNASTY. Mandragora, 1999.

"Cosimo De' Medici, Lord of Florence." The Medici Family. Accessed August 12, 2021. https://www.themedicifamily.com/Cosimo-de-Medici.html.

Durant, W. THE RENAISSANCE: THE STORY OF CIVILIZATION. Simon & Schuster, 2011.

"Execution of Girolamo Savonarola | History today." History Today |. n.d. https://www.historytoday.com/archive/months-past/execution-girolamo-savonarola

"The Florentine army, c.1260-1325 by Guy Halsall." Index - Illustrations of Costume & Soldiers. n.d. https://warfare.gq/13/Florence.htm

"Guild Information Packet." Fermilab Science Education Office. Accessed August 9, 2021. https://ed.fnal.gov/lincon/f97/projects/guildhall/guilds/guildinfo.html

"Guilded in Florence." The Florentine. Last modified March 21, 2007. https://www.theflorentine.net/2007/03/22/guilded-in-florence/.

"How the Medici Family's Influences Are Still Felt Today." Guide. Last modified April 19, 2017. https://www.sbs.com.au/guide/article/2017/04/19/how-medici-familys-influences-are-still-felt-today.

"John Hawkwood." Medieval Chronicles. n.d. https://www.medievalchronicles.com/medieval-knights/famous-medieval-knights/john-hawkwood/

"The Life and Reign of Catherine de Medici, Renaissance Queen." ThoughtCo. Accessed August 28, 2021. https://www.thoughtco.com/catherine-de-medici-biography-4155305

"Martin Luther's 95 Theses." Www.luther.de. Accessed August 28, 2021. https://www.luther.de/en/95thesen.html

"Medici Tomb Slab." Figuring the Unfigurable. Last modified August 14, 2014. https://figuringtheunfigurable.wordpress.com/2014/08/05/medici-tomb-slab/

"Pazzi conspiracy - Failed murder attempt on Lorenzo de Medici made him even more powerful and threw Renaissance Florence into chaos | Ancient pages." Ancient Pages. Last modified April 28, 2021. https://www.ancientpages.com/2021/04/28/pazzi-conspiracy-failed-murder-attempt-on-lorenzo-de-medici-made-him-even-more-powerful-and-threw-renaissance-florence-into-chaos/

"Warfare in Renaissance Italy." Weapons and Warfare. Last modified August 1, 2016. https://weaponsandwarfare.com/2016/08/02/warfare-in-renaissance-italy/.

"What is the Dome in Florence Called?" Mvorganizing.org – Knowledge Bank: Quick Advice for Everyone. Accessed August 12, 2021. https://www.mvorganizing.org/what-is-the-dome-in-florence-called/

Made in the USA
Middletown, DE
30 April 2024